THE 90% READING GOAL

90% of our students will read at
or above grade level
by the end of third grade

Lynn Fielding • **Nancy Kerr** • **Paul Rosier**

The Kennewick School Board, 1998
Kathleen Daily
Ed Frost
Lynn Fielding
John Hodge
Dan Mildon

Kennewick is located in southeastern Washington where the Columbia, Snake, and Yakima rivers meet. With neighboring cities Pasco and Richland, it forms the Tri-Cities, the largest metropolitan area between Portland and Spokane. Each city has its own government and school system. With the adjacent smaller communities of Benton City, Burbank, Connell, Finley, and Prosser, the urban area has a population of 165,000 and thirty-nine elementary schools. Kennewick serves 14,000 students in thirteen full-sized elementary schools, four middle schools and three high schools. Seventeen percent of Kennewick's students are ethnic minorities; thirty-nine percent are eligible for government lunch programs. Its general operation budget is $83 million.

The New Foundation Press
2527 W. Kennewick Ave. #313
Kennewick, Wa 99336
Phone/Fax: (509) 783-5237

Kennewick School District: http://www.ksd.org
The Reading Foundation: http//www.readingfoundation.org

Library of Congress Catalogue Card Number: 98-092009
ISBN: 0-9666875-0-7
Printed in the United States of America

The following are registered trademarks: Distar, Dr. Seuss, Nancy Drew, Hardy Boys, Garfield, Reading Recovery, Spiderman, and Success for All.

To Wendy, Leland, and Mary,

and

To the teachers and administrators
of the Kennewick Schools,
who together are making it happen,
one child at a time.

Acknowledgements

To quote a sports T-shirt, "We are born alone, we die alone, but in between we play on teams." This book is the result of a team effort, and we wish to acknowledge those contributions while accepting full responsibility for the final product.

Our spouses and families have been wonderfully supportive and understanding of the drain of time and resources necessary to put this many words together in a coherent fashion. They have offered a variety of improvements to the text as well.

Early drafts were reviewed by Terry Barber, Deb Bowen, Greg Fancher, Claudia Glover, Ian Lamont, Marlis Lindbloom, A. Melody, Steve Nielsen (WSSDA), Terry Tannenberg, and Gregg Wishkoski, as well as by Kennewick School Board members Kathleen Daily, Ed Frost, John Hodge, and Dan Mildon. These reviewers generously offered advice about an evolving product, expressing faith in the final outcome.

We express special thanks to Rose Thompson for the countless details she cheerfully and competently managed, to our editor, Lavina Fielding Anderson, and our designer/typesetter, Melani St. John, for their professional skills, and to Mary Ann Lush, our representative at Publishers Press, who faciliated the production.

Like the proverbial elephant, the "90% goal" seems different from different points of view. It may feel like a rope to swing on for the children at its tail, a pointed spear for principals feeling its tusk, another trendy flap in educational winds for professional institutions feeling the ears, and a rough tree trunk to climb for teachers and parents feeling its legs. But this is a baby elephant. It is still growing. Most of the insights in this book came out of classrooms, committees, and workshops from scores of teachers and administrators in Kennewick. To them we express our greatest gratitude.

CONTENTS

We can eliminate illiteracy in our society. We can do this by eradicating below grade level reading achievement in our first, second, and third grades.

We can eliminate illiteracy when our school districts publicly commit to teach 90% of their students to read at grade level by third grade, then systematically realign their assessments, curriculum, instructional time, reporting systems, and available resources to achieve this goal.

We can eliminate illiteracy nationwide in four to seven years:

90% of third graders reading at or above grade level.

INTRODUCTION

THE 90%
READING GOAL

*"Sometimes a truth is so simple and obvious
that it eludes detection for years."*

—Dan Yankelovich[1]

A child who doesn't read has little chance to succeed. For the past two hundred years, the printed and digital word has increasingly permeated social and economic life. A child who doesn't read, or who reads poorly, must endure nine to twelve years in an educational system that uses reading as its primary delivery system. As an adult, he or she must function in an economic system where the transfer of information by reading is exponentially rewarded and, conversely, where lack of that ability is punished.

We all want our children to read. We want 90% or more to read well by third grade. Yet nationwide, 40% of America's children do not read well,[2] and about 25% read so poorly that they enter the fourth grade reading at a first- and second-grade level. They are effectively banished to the fringes of our information society by age nine.

Most school board members and parents think that 90% of children in their local schools perform near grade level in this most basic skill. Most

---

[1] Dan Yankelovich, "How Public Opinion Really Works," *Fortune Magazine*, October 1992. Yankelovich is cofounder, with former Secretary of State Cyrus Vance, of Public Agenda, the nonprofit research foundation that published the seminal educational research *First Things First* in 1994.

[2] National Assessment of Educational Progress, *NAEP 1996 Trends in Academic Progress* (Washington, DC: National Center for Educational Statistics, 1997), 104; America's Reading Challenge, U.S. Department of Education, Region X, Office of Public Affairs, 1/15/97.

legislators and newspaper publishers assume that all but inner-city schools send third graders into fourth grade reading at grade level.

But our elementary teachers and principals know better. In most of our own communities, they think that it is utterly impossible to teach 90% of third graders to read at grade level.

Each of these groups is shocked by the reaction of the other. How can those in charge of public education routinely assume that most children—90% or more—read at grade level, while educators not only know they are not but also think that this level of literacy is impossible to achieve?

This chasm between the public perception and educational achievement levels of our children is the core of the reading crisis.

How to bring current levels of achievement up to the current levels of public perception is the focus of this book. This book is written for school board members, superintendents, legislators, newspaper editors, and parents. It is not abstract, theoretical, or particularly gentle. The ideas are simple, and our approach is pragmatic and blunt.

We describe the single-minded and passionate commitment of educators in one school district, in one state, to one goal: that 90% of our children will read at or above grade level by the end of their third-grade year. We are approaching this goal in Kennewick. In May 1996, we were at 55%—in May 1998, at 71%. Of thirteen full-sized elementary schools, two scored above 90% and three others scored in the high 70s and low 80s.

We will tell you why we chose this goal, how we are achieving it, and how you can replicate it. We will describe the creation and growth of the Reading Foundation, a nonprofit organization that encourages parents to read with their children from birth twenty minutes a day. This organization can also be duplicated in your community.

This is a plan which will work in all 15,000 school districts across America's fifty states.[3] Some of those districts are tiny with only a few hundred students. Others are huge with hundreds of thousands of students. Regardless of size, the children in all of these districts have the same need. They need to learn to read.

---

[3] Thomas D. Snyder, Charlene M. Hoffman, and Claire M. Geddes, *Digest of Education Statistics* 1997 (Washington, DC: U.S. Department of Education, National Center for Education Statistics, 1997), 54, 96. In the United States in 1995-96, 44.8 million students were taught in 14,883 public school districts, with 3.3 to 3.6 million students at each grade until they begin dropping out in high school. In 1995-96, 769 (5.2%) of the districts with enrollments of 10,000 or more students taught 49.1% of our students; 1,013 districts with enrollment between 5,000 to 9,999 taught 15.7% of our students, and 2,027 districts enrolling between 2,500 to 4,999 taught 16.0% of our students. In short, 3,809 (25.6%) districts serve 80.8% of public school students.

This book does not recommend any instructional approach. It does not tell teachers how to teach reading. It is written to those with the political power and responsibility to assure that public education works. It is about adult accountability, system accountability, and results. It is not about instruction. It is about proper governance.

This is not an "us" and "them" process. We are all in this together. Throughout this book, we three authors refer to the goal—to teach 90% of our children to read by third grade—as "our goal" and its challenges as those "we" can overcome. It is not an accusation or an advertisement. It is an invitation.

This book explains:

- How we as board members and superintendents can decide that 90% of third graders in our district will read at or above grade level within the next four to seven years, and how to create the policies, tests, reports, staff training, and reallocation of resources to make it happen.

- How our legislators can extend reading accountability state-wide.

- How our newspaper publishers can assure the next generation of adult literacy in their communities.

- How our parents can help each of their children acquire this skill.

A Reality Check

Reading is our first and most basic educational process. From kindergarten through third grade, children learn to read. Thereafter they read to learn. Children who read well by third grade do well in our schools. Children who do not learn to read well by third grade do poorly. Sometimes they do poorly for the rest of their lives. This is something we all know.

Part 1 explains:

- Why we need to focus on reading (Chapters 1-2)
- What happens when we don't (Chapters 3-4)
- How the 90% reading goal works (Chapters 5-7)
- How to involve families (Chapter 8)
- How to invite community participation (Chapter 9)

At 300 words a minute and skipping nothing from the title page to the back cover, you can read this entire book in 3 hours and 27 minutes. Part 1, including sidebars, kickers, and footnotes, will take 1 hour and 32 minutes.

CHAPTER ONE

IMAGINE OPENING THE DOOR

"There is always one moment in childhood when the door opens and lets the future in."

—Graham Green

Every day some children, for the first time in their whole lives, see the door crack open. Beyond is a brilliant world. It is not the world they feel and smell and hear and touch. It is a symbolic world which they can share with the best storytellers, generals, athletes, and poets, –with the best scientists, mathematicians, and historians of the past three millennia. It is the pulsating world of computer screens and business contracts and freeway signs and coliseum seating. It is baseball cards and comic strips and the backs of cereal boxes. It is Dr. Seuss, Garfield and Spiderman, Nancy Drew and the Hardy Boys.

For about 40% of our children, the door opens fairly easily. The required brain development and social preconditioning come together smoothly. For another 30-40% of our children, it requires significantly more effort. And for the remaining 20-30%, opening that door may be one of the most difficult tasks of their life.[1] So difficult, in fact, that many of them never walk

---

[1] G. Reid Lyon, Ph.D., Chief of the Child Development and Behavior Branch of the National Institute of Child Health and Human Development (NICHD) National Institutes of Health (NIH), *Statement before the Committee of Labor and Human Resources, United States Senate, Washington, D.C., Tuesday, April 28, 1998*, 1. Because of its clarity and completeness, this statement is reproduced in full in Appendix B. The NICHD supports research at 41 sites in North America, Europe, and Asia analyzing the conditions that foster strong reading development, risk factors that predispose youngsters to failure, and early instruction procedures to ameliorate reading deficits.

through that door. Yet when the reading door does not open, hundreds of other doors leading to exciting, financially rewarding, and personally fulfilling worlds also remain shut.

Extraordinary doors open after the reading door is opened. Years after he stepped through the reading door, Neil Armstrong stepped on the moon. Walt Disney and Steven Spielberg each invented their fantasy worlds after

Fig. 1.1. How we deliver 85% of the curriculum[2]

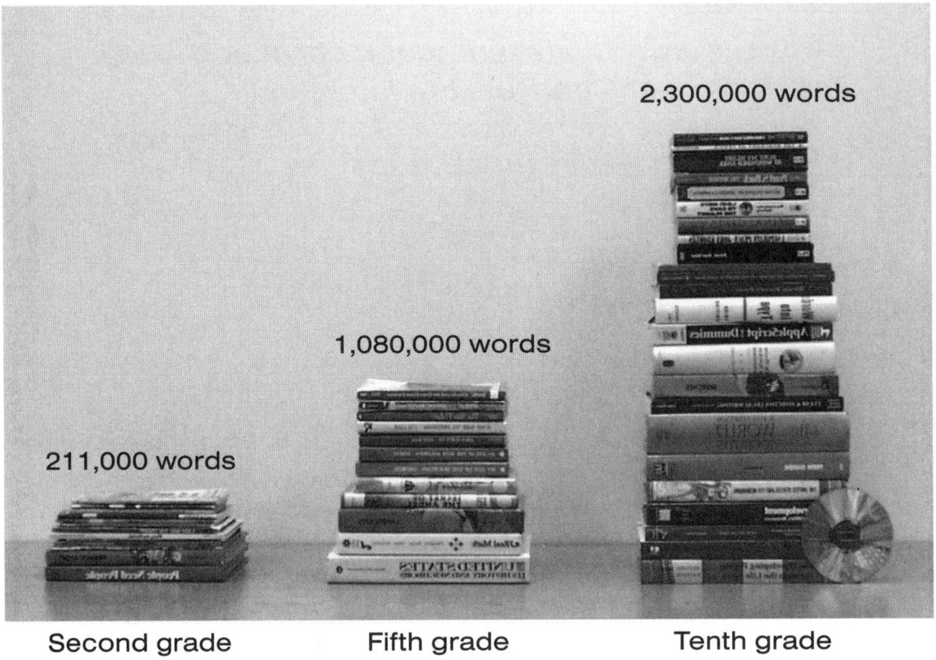

211,000 words — Second grade
1,080,000 words — Fifth grade
2,300,000 words — Tenth grade

they entered the reading world. Imagine if Oprah Winfrey or Larry King could not read. Imagine the limitations on your minister or lawyer or dentist or physician if he or she, as a skinny kid losing front teeth at age six, seven, and eight, had not learned to read.

Reading is not a content area like math, science, literature, or social studies. Reading is a skill. It is the process skill by which children get informa-

---

[2] Curriculum varies immensely between classrooms even at the second grade and even more because of the elective courses by high school. These numbers are conservative estimates derived with the aid of Judy Wentz and Sharon Frymier at Lincoln Elementary and the staff at Kennewick High.

tion from blackboards, books, and computer screens to learn math, science, literature, and social studies. It is the skill directly related to 85% of all adult economic activity.[3] It is the skill upon which we rely in the public schools to transmit 85% of our curriculum.[4]

Reading is a prerequisite for most adult employment, for personal fulfillment, and for a continued democracy.

When we as school board members and superintendents look at discipline, attendance, self-esteem, and drop-out problems in our schools, we are looking for the most part at children who do not read at grade level. When we as parents and legislators look at juvenile criminality and gang activity, we are generally looking at kids with poorly functioning symbolic skills. Poverty, incarceration, crime, and violence all have a common denominator in our society.[5] That commonality is exclusion. Most of these children grew into adulthood unable to read in an information society.[6]

These children are disabled by the malfunctioning of the same community institution—our first three grades of school. Our public schools do a good job of opening the world to 60% of our children and an exceptional

"Forty percent of all children are now reading below the basic level on national reading assessments. Children who cannot read early and well are hampered at the very start of their education—and for the rest of their lives. This will be even truer as we move into the 21st century. To participate in America's high-skill workplaces, to cruise—much less use—the Internet, all children need to read better than ever before." [7]

---

[3] By the year 2000, 85% of employment will require skilled or professional levels of training. U.S. Bureau of Labor, as qtd. in *Final Report: Governor's Council on School-to-Work Transition* (Olympia, WA: State of Washington, March 1995), 4. Almost all of this training requires the ability to read well.

[4] "In the United States, an estimated 85% of classroom time spent on instruction involves using textbooks." João Oliveria, "Textbooks in Developing Countries," in *Promoting Reading in Developing Countries,* edited by Vincent Greaney (Washington, DC: World Bank, 1996), 78, citing L. Anderson, "The Environment of Instruction: The Function of Seatwork in a Commercially Developed Curriculum," in *Comprehension Instruction: Perspective and Suggestions,* edited by G. G. Duffy, L. R. Roehler, and J. Mason (White Plains, NY: Longman, 1984), 93-103; and State of Florida, *Instructional Materials Committee on Training Materials* (Tallahassee, FL: State of Florida Department of Education, 1993).

[5] Orton Dyslexia Society, "Some Facts about Illiteracy in America," *Perspectives on Dyslexia* 13, no. 4 (1988): 1-13, cited in J. W. Lerner, "Theories for Intervention in Reading," in *Reading and the Special Learner,* edited by C. N. Hedley and J. S. Hicks, (Norwood, NJ: Ablex Publishing, 1988), 7-20.

[6] "This is the information age," says Bill Gates. Computing is not yet the largest industry in the world—at $360 billion a year it runs behind autos and oil—but it has become the most important because of its power to transform the way people work. Stratford Sherman, "The New Computer Revolution," *Fortune,* June 14, 1993, 56-76. Computer systems are 25% of all capital equipment purchases. *Businessweek,* Nov. 1993, 22.

[7] "President Clinton's America's Reading Challenge," flier, U.S. Department of Education, Region X, Office of Public Affairs, Jan. 15, 1997.

job with the upper 10%. We need only compare the academic performance of the highest performing seniors in 1948 with the similar group of seniors in 1998 to see systemic growth.[8] But the improvement has not been uniform. It has not assured uniform mastery of the basic skill of reading for all children.

> "In school lore, second grade is broadly viewed as children's last chance. Those who are not on track by third grade have little chance of ever catching up."[9]

The harshest handicap we can impose on children in our public schools is to fail to teach them by third grade to read well. When we fail, the child fails. We create for her or him a cycle of continued failure, diminished self-esteem, lowered self-expectations, and decreased effort. It does not matter what book we hand to a child who does not read. The door is shut.

The most complicated burden we place on our education system grows out of our failure to teach students by third grade to read well and at grade level.

- We create an immense and nearly unmanageable learning span within each classroom. How well can we address the expectations of parents and the needs of their children in a fourth-grade classroom learning science when 25% of the class reads below second-grade level and 25% reads above fifth-grade level?
- We create a core of predictably and increasingly unmotivated, inattentive, and unruly students who are four and five times more likely to be referred to the office for discipline infractions by sixth grade, than those reading at or above grade level. (See Chapter 4.) We then divert a disproportionate amount of staff and administrative time away from academic issues to deal with these disruptions.
- We create the pool from which most of our drop-outs emerge.

The most expensive burden we place on our society is those students we have failed to teach to read well. The silent army of low readers who move through our schools, siphoning off the lion's share of administrative resources, emerge into society as adults still lacking the single prerequisite for managing their lives and acquiring additional training.

- They are chronically unemployed, underemployed, or unemployable.

---

[8] For a discussion of significant system improvement, see D. Berliner and B. Biddle, *The Manufactured Crisis: Myths, Fraud, and the Attack on America's Public Schools* (Reading, MA: Addison-Wesley, 1997).

[9] Catherine E. Snow, M. Susan Burns, and Peg Griffin, eds., *Preventing Reading Difficulties in Young Children* (Washington, DC: National Research Council/National Academy Press, 1998), 212.

- They form the single largest identifiable group of those whom we incarcerate, and to whom we provide public assistance, housing, medical care, and other social services.
- They perpetuate and enlarge the problem by creating another generation of poor readers.

These problems have other roots too, but teaching children to read well strikes at a persistent, recurring, and primary cause. We will never effectively deal with the repetitive spiral of underemployment, poverty, violent crime, and personal pain until we deal with its principal root: the inability to read. Thus, in our search for academic solutions for academic problems we may find an academic solution to our most pressing social problems.

The reading door is closed to 25% of our children and almost closed for another 15%. Imagine opening it.

CHAPTER TWO

RESOLVING TO OPEN THE DOOR

"We can affect the lives of more children, more deeply, for a longer period of time, at less cost, by teaching them to read well by third grade, than by any other single thing we can do in our school systems."

—Kathleen Daily, Kennewick School Board

In 1961 a doubting nation listened as President John F. Kennedy announced a bold national goal: The United States would land a man on the moon and return him safely to the Earth by the end of the decade.

Standing on the moon was the fantasy of sci-fi movies and comic books, of Greek myths and childhood dreams. Most people thought it was impossible. Yet, with national pride and perhaps survival at stake, the entire country embraced the goal. Great leaders stimulated new solutions and reallocated resources. It was an impossible goal . . . and we did it.

"We choose to go to the moon! We choose to go to the moon in this decade and do the other things—not because they are easy, but because they are hard. Because that goal will serve to organize and measure the best of our abilities and skills, because that challenge is one that we are willing to accept, one we are unwilling to postpone, and one which we intend to win."

—President John F. Kennedy[1]

---

[1] President John F. Kennedy, Rice University, Sept. 12, 1962, qtd. in Harry Hurt III, *For All Mankind* (New York: Atlantic Monthly Press, 1988), xi.

Today the reading goal is an educational "moon shot." It may seem impossible. But with a national effort, it can be done. It must be done if we are going to hold our place in the economic world of the twenty-first century. As visionary and capable leaders champion the goal, as we realign our tremendous human and monetary resources, and as we aim toward the clear, specific target, we will achieve the impossible dream. America's children will read early and will read well.

> "We must hold both schools and students accountable for learning, not just for following all the rules or sitting through the required number of classes. We will not break our promise to raise academic standards. Every third grader must read at the third-grade level, and every high school graduate must master basic academic skills and knowledge."
>
> —Governor Gary Locke (D)
> State of Washington
> Inaugural Address, January 15, 1997

> "You cannot succeed if you cannot read. All Texas children must learn the one skill that can make all the difference in their lives: reading. That is why I set the clearest and most profound goal I have for Texas: that every child, each and every child, should learn to read at grade level by the third grade and continue reading at grade level or better throughout his or her public school career."
>
> —Governor George W. Bush (R), State of Texas, State of the State Address January 28, 1997

Of all the educational issues clamoring for attention, this one evokes nearly universal acceptance and priority because of its immense leverage. With a high degree of assurance, we can teach more children to read at grade level by third grade, at a fraction of the social cost to the child and the economic cost to our society, than by teaching them to read when they are middle school students, high school students, or adults.

Of the children who leave third grade reading below grade level, 74% never catch up.[2]

Seven Reasons to Set a Goal

We can capture the imagination and mobilize the resources of our districts, states, and nation with a clear child-centered goal. Here are seven good reasons why we as legislators, superintendents, school board members, publishers, and/or parents should lead the efforts to establish the reading goal in our jurisdictions.

---

[2]"Seventy-four percent of children who are poor readers in the third grade remain poor readers in the ninth grade." D. J. Francis, S. E. Shaywitz, K. K. Stuebing, B. A. Shaywitz, and J. M. Fletcher, "Developmental Lag Versus Deficit Models of Reading Disability: A Longitudinal, Individual Growth Curves Analysis," *Journal of Educational Psychology* 88, no. 1 (1966): 3-17.

1. **The goal is powered by true vision.** It strikes at the root of our most basic educational problem. It creates a primary focus and educational priority. All academic subjects and skills are not equal. Reading is paramount, and reading well by the third grade is essential. With few exceptions, seniors graduating with high achievements are those reading proficiently nine years earlier.[3] Elementary reading is our greatest educational challenge. When we meet it, we solve many of its related problems.

2. **The goal offers immense rewards.** It is what every parent and grandparent wants for his or her child and grandchild, what every employer needs in an employee, and what every student needs for a productive life. Can our billion dollar education industry, together with parents and businesses in each community, reach beyond where we have ever reached before? In the challenge to create a world-class educational system, it is the first outpost. It raises education to a whole new level.

3. **The goal is clear.** The public understands its specific language—90%, third grade. It is clear because it is measurable and accountable. Parents, principals, teachers, and taxpayers alike can understand where their elementary school is in relationship to the goal, chart their school's annual progress, and know when their school reaches the goal.

4. **The goal is compassionate.** The children who are truly at risk in this world are those who cannot read. There is no fairer or more even start than providing public school students with the single basic academic skill necessary to access information for the rest of their lives. The cycles of poverty, crime, and personal

> *"Recent studies conclude that 85 to 90% of even our poorest readers can be taught to read at grade level. The commitment of Success for All is to do whatever it takes to see that every child makes it through third grade at or near grade level in reading."*
>
> —Robert Slavin[4]

---

[3] The Commission on Reading of the National Academy of Education points out: "While a country receives a good return on investment in education at all levels from nursery school and kindergarten through college, the research reveals that the returns are highest from the early years of schooling when children are first learning to read. The Commission on Excellence warned of the risk for America from shortcomings in secondary education. Yet the early years set the stage for later learning. Without the ability to read, excellence in high school and beyond is unattainable." Richard C. Anderson, Elfrieda H. Hiebert, Judith A. Scott, and Ian A. G. Wilkinson, *Becoming a Nation of Readers: The Report of the Commission on Reading* (Champaign-Urbana, IL: Center for the Study of Reading, 1985), 1.

[4] Robert Slavin is the co-director, Center for Research on the Education of Children Placed at Risk, Johns Hopkins University, and one of the cofounders of the Success for All program, 1998.

pain will continue to recur for those whom we condemn to live surrounded by information they cannot access.

5. **The goal mobilizes a virtual army of educators.** As a result of declaring the goal, a powerful shift occurs in our districts' and our states' elementary schools. Principals and our most responsive teachers begin refocusing time, curriculum, and structure on what moves their students toward the visible and measurable 90% goal. Most third-grade classrooms will see a 10-15% gain just by increasing the amount of time spent on reading and decreasing time spent elsewhere. Deeper, secondary gains will require curricular and organizational changes—in kindergarten through third grade and through the intentional involvement of parents.

6. **The goal provides early and continual wins.** The nation's moon shot was a one-time, do-or-die proposition. Local districts' educational moonshot will provide local focus each September and local wins each May as we tabulate and report district gains. Almost every elementary school will be able to achieve an annual 6-10% growth toward the goal. And if a building or a district makes only half of the 8-12% annual growth necessary to reach the goal in four to seven years, there is still a silver lining. Because of the goal, thousands of additional children will progress across the reading threshold.

> "We have learned that for 90% to 95% of poor readers, prevention and early intervention programs that combine instruction in phoneme awareness, phonics, fluency development, and reading comprehension strategies, provided by well-trained teachers, can increase reading skills to average reading levels. However, we have also learned that if we delay intervention until nine years of age (the time that most children with reading difficulties receive services), approximately 75% of the children will continue to have difficulties learning to read throughout high school. To be clear, while older children and adults can be taught to read, the time and expense of doing so is enormous."
>
> —G. Reid Lyon[5]

---

[5] G. Reid Lyon, Ph.D., Chief of the Child Development and Behavior Branch of the National Institute of Child Health and Human Development (NICHD) National Institutes of Health (NIH), *Statement before the Committee of Labor and Human Resources, United States Senate, Washington, D.C., Tuesday, April 28, 1998,* reproduced in Appendix B.

7. **The goal produces wonderful yet unintended results.**

    - School boards, legislators, and professional educator groups can unite in support of our basic academic purpose instead of splitting over the many social issues on which we do not agree.

    - We can stop giving energy to the unwinnable battle between phonics vs. whole language. (See Appendix F.) Instead of continuing the debate over what is "theoretically consistent," we can refocus on "what works." Teachers can develop a greater repertoire of approaches to match the different learning needs of children.

    - The focus on reading-results almost automatically generates the long-sought-for parent/school partnership. Teachers, now accountable, energetically and naturally enlist parents to read with their children at home.

    - Families will be strengthened. As children snuggle under the arms and into the laps of their parents and other care-givers to read, many toddlers and preschoolers will double or triple the daily amount of positive attention they receive from adults.

> *"We now have converging research that tells us that reading problems are preventable and they are preventable in most children. We know enough to mitigate factors of poor home environment, second language, and low socioeconomic environment. With proper first teaching, continual assessment, and immediate adjustment of teaching strategies when indicated, 80% of first graders can read first-grade material by the middle of first grade; 85% to 95% of third graders can read at grade level by the end of third grade."*
>
> —Linda Diamond, Vice President, Consortium for Reading Excellence, 1998

CHAPTER THREE

DISMANTLING THE ILLUSION

---

*The great illusion: 90% of the third graders in my
district already read at grade level.*

PRETEST
Circle the correct answer.

1. What percentage of children in your district, community, or state do you want to read at grade level
   when they enter the fourth grade?

   a. About 40%

   b. About 60%

   c. More than 90%

2. In your opinion, what percentage of children in your
   district, community, or state actually read at grade
   level when they enter the fourth grade?

   a. 55% or less

   b. 65-75%

   c. 80%

   d. 90%

3. In your opinion, what percentage of children in your district, community, or state actually read at a first- or second-grade level upon entering the fourth grade?
   a. 10%
   b. 20%
   c. 25%
   d. 35%
4. On what information do you base these opinions?

If your school district is typical, the correct answers are:

1. (c) 90%
2. (a) 55% or less
3. (c) 25%
4. decades of poorly understood statistical reports.

In order to dismantle the great illusion around reading, we need to take a look at actual student performance levels. By the beginning of third grade, children read on as many as eight different grade levels, as illustrated by the chart of the reading levels of Kennewick students at the beginning of third grade in 1995. (See Fig. 3.1 and Appendix C, which contains the raw scores school by school from which the range is summarized.) This range in scores is typical of third graders in districts whose average score is between the 35th and 65th percentiles on nationally normed tests.

> "The range of academic performance within each grade is always greater than the range between each grade. Our data show that the range within each grade for math is seldom less than five years and for reading is seldom less than seven years."
>
> —Allan Olson, Executive Director
> Northwest Evaluation Association

Most third-grade classrooms in each of our nation's 15,000 districts have this range in reading ability. If our district scores in the 35th percentile, it simply means that we have more students reading in the lower ranges, lowering the average. If our district scores in the 65th percentile, we still have this eight-year span. We just have more students reading in the higher levels, raising the average. Data from the Northwest Evaluation Association, a national testing and research organization, indicates that the range persists regardless of the overall district averages. The difference within grades is always greater than the difference between grades.[1]

---

[1] The same variation can also be seen in vocabulary size. First graders' speaking vocabularies range from 5,500 to 32,000 words. Twelfth graders' vocabularies range from 28,200 to 73,200 words. The vocabularies of some first graders exceed those of some twelfth graders. M. Smith, "Measurement of the Size of General English Vocabulary Through the Elementary Grades and High School," *Genetic Psychology Monographs* 24 (1941): 311-45.

If our district scores between the 40th and 60th percentile on a standardized nationally normed test, it is fairly accurate to visualize about 15% of the third graders reading at each of the eight grade levels, with a slight bulge at the third grade (23%) as Figure 3.1 shows, and a sharper tapering at the sixth, seventh and eighth grades. It is not accurate to visualize most of the third graders in our districts closely clustered around the third-grade level.

Children on the low end of this eight-grade reading span may barely recognize letters. On the upper end of the span, readers comprehend specialized vocabularies describing complex or contradictory relationships. Because remediation is so ineffective, the reading span persists nationally within each grade through high school.

This differentiated reading ability contributes significantly to—even drives—most educational problems. The range in students' basic ability to learn from the printed word explains the continued clustering of problems that seem resistant to every other nonreading solution. Low-reading students persist in low academic achievement despite self-esteem building, heterogeneous grouping, and other interventions.

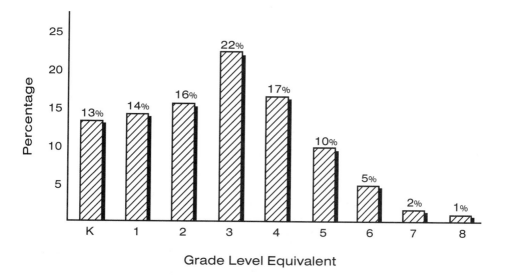

Fig. 3.1
Kennewick School District's
Third Grade Reading Skill Distribution
Fall 1995

Poor readers will continue to be low academic achievers until they learn to read.

It is difficult to imagine a contrary result. Our nation's lowest fourth-graders read 30-100 words a minute with a first- and second-grade vocabulary and comprehension. Our highest fourth-graders read 200-300 words a minute with vocabulary and comprehension typical of the sixth, seventh, and eighth grades.[2] During the fourth grade, the top 10% of children in each class read and comprehend ten times more words than the children in the bottom 10%. In addition, the upper groups typically read much more outside of class, thereby forging ahead even faster. The lower groups spend almost no time reading outside of class, falling even farther behind.

> "What we as educators never tell our public is that one in four children enters the fourth grade reading at a first- or second-grade level. We can often sit on a school board for a decade before we realize this ourselves."
>
> —Lynn Fielding, Kennewick School Board

Board members, legislators, parents, and newspaper publishers rarely see this eight-grade reading span in the national standardized test reports. The usual formats for presenting student academic achievement are percentiles, stanines, and quartiles, all of which measure low-performing third graders against average-performing third graders. Percentiles, stanines, and quartiles give no information about how the low-performing third graders compare with the average-performing second graders or average-performing first graders. We get little information from statistical measures of the eight-year reading span.

And we rarely, if ever, see charts converting the percentile rankings to grade-level equivalents. When that information is provided about the low-performing individual students, often all the information below (and above) certain points is collapsed into a single category so that the report shows only a four- or five-year spread in scores, not a seven- or eight-year spread. A third-grade child with kindergarten level skills who can barely sound out letters and who scores in the first (lowest) percentile is almost never reported as reading at a kindergarten or first-grade level.

An alternative and more accurate reporting format for children reading below the truncation point would code these readers with a symbol like an

---

[2] Richard C. Anderson, P. T. Wilson, and L. G. Fielding, "Growth in Reading and How Children Spend Their Time Outside of School," *Reading Research Quarterly* 23 (1988): 285-303; and Richard C. Anderson, "Research Foundations to Support Wide Reading," in *Promoting Reading in Developing Countries*, edited by Vincent Greaney (New York: International Reading Association, 1992), 66.

asterisk (*), keyed to the explanation: "This child reads below the levels that this test can accurately measure."

What happens in our districts when the reading proficiency of the lowest 25% in every group of students tested is either over-reported or masked by statistical measures?

- Parents watching their own child struggle rarely can identify reading as the problem. The test scores, coupled with reassurances that "he'll catch up" and "kids learn at different rates," mask the truly desperate nature of the problem. After all, "someone has to be in the 20th percentile," and second grade/sixth month is only "a little behind." So parents who would move heaven and earth to help their child, don't hire a tutor, don't read daily with their child, and don't seek other assistance.

Children Seldom Catch Up

- *"More than eight of ten children with severe word reading problems at the end of first grade performed below the average range at the beginning of third grade."* [3]

- *Children who fall behind in first grade have a one in eight chance of ever catching up to grade level without extraordinary efforts.* [4]

- *"Eighty-eight percent of children who were deficient in word recognition skills in the first grade were poor readers in fourth grade."* [5]

- *"Seventy-four percent of children who are poor readers in the third grade remain poor readers in the ninth grade."* [6]

- 15,000 local school boards remain immobilized. The President of the United States may highlight reading as the number one educational initiative, but most board members can honestly say, "We've seen the numbers in our district. Where is the crisis?"

- Newspaper publishers and legislators never see the eight-year reading span within each grade level and look elsewhere for educational improvement.

---

[3] J. K. Torgesen, R. K. Wagner, and C. A. Rashotte, "Prevention and Remediation of Severe Reading Disabilities: Keeping the End in Mind," *Scientific Studies of Reading 1* (1997): 217-34.

[4] C. Juel, *Learning to Read and Write in One Elementary School* (New York: Springer-Verlag, 1994): 120.

[5] C. Juel, "Learning to Read and Write: A Longitudinal Study of 54 Children from First Through Fourth Grades," *Journal of Educational Psychology* 80, no. 4 (1988): 437-47.

[6] D. J. Francis, S. E. Shaywitz, K. K. Stuebing, B. A. Shaywitz, and J. M. Fletcher, "Developmental Lag Versus Deficit Models of Reading Disability: A Longitudinal, Individual Growth Curves Analysis," *Journal of Educational Psychology* 88, no. 1 (1996): 3-17.

When we have bad information, or not all the information, we make serious mistakes. When we cannot see the eight-year reading range or when our lowest fourth-grade child is reported as reading only a year and four months away from grade level, we focus our attention elsewhere as we seek school improvement. The primary reason sixteen years of school reform has focused almost   everywhere except on elementary reading is that decision-makers get information that masks how poorly the lowest 25% of our children read.

The 1994 National Assessment of Educational Progress (NAEP)[7] illustrates a similar range of reading abilities. On a 500-point range test, the range for fourth, eighth, and twelfth graders between the 10th and 90th percentile was:

Grade	Low	Average	High
4th	159	219	263
8th	211	262	305
12th	239	290	332

The fourth-, eighth-, and twelfth-grade tests were scaled to test certain kinds of reading stances (reading for literacy experience, reading for information, reading to perform a task) with similar questions at the same points on the scale using grade-level appropriate material.

When we as board members, superintendents, legislators, newspaper publishers, and parents discern the tremendous range in reading abilities by third grade and the predictable classroom failure at every level of those who read poorly, it is clear that we can change the lives of these children more profoundly for less money by teaching them to read early and well than by any other single thing we do.

---

[7] Educational Testing Service under contract with the National Center for Education Statistics, *NAEP 1994 Reading Report Card for the Nation and the States* (Washington, DC: National Center for Education Statistics, Office of Educational Research and Improvement, U.S. Department of Education, Jan. 1996), 93-94.

CHAPTER FOUR

THE FACE OF A CHILD

"Skilled readers do well in our society. This is true from the time they start their first job as students until they retire from jobs in business and industry six decades later. Unskilled readers struggle in our society. They struggle every time they come in contact with print."

—Gregg Wishkoski, President
Kennewick Education Association, 1997-99

Statistics, facts, and figures reveal only half of the toll of illiteracy. The other half occurs deep in the hearts and lives of our children. In this chapter you will meet Mindy and Tony, two composite children reflecting thousands of recurring real life stories.

NOW

Fourth graders are nine-going-on-ten years old. They weigh 50 to 70 pounds. They come in a vast array of colors, sizes, and shapes. Tony is one of them, and he can't read. Actually, he can read. He reads on a first grade/sixth month level but he is staring blankly at his science book. It's from a national publisher, carefully written on a fourth-grade level.

> So scientists believe that there never was any water on the moon. The moon is a dry, airless, and very barren place.

This is what the sentence looks like to adults like you and me with high school diplomas and college degrees. It's what the sentence looks like to

Mindy, sitting next to Tony. To Tony, who struggles to decipher: "See the cat" the sentence looks like:

So scxxxxxsts bexxxve that there never was any wxxer on the moon. The moon is a drx, axxxss, and very bxxxn place.

Or, more realistically, because we adults fluently recognize the repetitive x's and other letters, it really looks more like:

Só §cioΩπsτs bσfiove rhaτ rhσ‣e nσvσ was aΩy waτσ‣ óΩ rhσ móóΩ. Γhσ móóΩ is a d‣▾, ai‣fσss and ve‣▾ ba‣‣σΩ pfaco.

Tony doesn't like science. Science is very hard. Math and social studies are hard, too. Tony knows that he can sit longer and work harder than Mindy, but he still won't get it.

Mindy gets it. She just looks at the pages and gets it. Tony doesn't know why. He doesn't know that Mindy's parents have read to her at least twenty minutes a day since birth and still do. He doesn't know that the happy accumulation of alphabet letters around the crib, pointing out the "S" on STOP signs, daytime reading, and bedtime stories have banked a solid investment of more than a thousand hours in Mindy's literacy skill before she came to kindergarten. She came ready to learn, and especially ready to learn to read.

Tony doesn't know that the curriculum in kindergarten, first, second, and third grades was especially geared for Mindy. Kindergarten focused on social skills, and first- and second-grade reading programs were designed for students who had spent their preschool years in symbol- saturated environments. Mindy is one of the 18% who reads at a fifth-through eighth-grade level by the beginning of third grade. And, unlike Tony, Mindy spends a lot of her free time with a book. (See Table 1.)

> "We have learned that just as many girls as boys have difficulties learning to read. Until five years ago, the conventional wisdom was that many more boys than girls had such difficulties. Now females should have equal access to screening and intervention programs."
>
> —G. Reid Lyon[1]

---

[1] G. Reid Lyon, Ph.D., Chief of the Child Development and Behavior Branch, National Institute of Child Health and Human Development, *Statement before the Committee of Labor and Human Resources, . . . 1998*, reproduced in Appendix B.

Table 1
Variation in Numbers of Minutes and Words
Read Outside of Class by Fifth Graders

Percentile Ranking	Minutes Reading Per Day	Words Read Per Year
98	65.0	4,358,000
90	21.2	1,823,000
80	14.2	1,146,000
70	9.6	622,000
60	6.5	432,000
50	4.6	282,000
40	3.2	200,000
30	1.8	106,000
20	.7	21,000
10	.1	8,000

Source: Richard C. Anderson, "Research Foundations to Support Wide Reading," in *Promoting Reading in Developing Countries*, edited by Vincent Greaney (New York: International Reading Association, 1992), 66.

Tony doesn't know that fundamentally different reading strategies would have been more appropriate for him as he labored through those same four years. He doesn't know that a twenty-minute test in kindergarten[2] could have accurately predicted his reading difficulty and indicated specific teaching strategies which Mindy does not need. The traditional amount of instructional time which worked so well for Mindy could not work for him. Tony doesn't know that his teachers have access to only three or four reading intervention strategies for him, generally used in third and fourth grade, when they really needed the flexibility of seven to ten strategies all the way through kindergarten, first, and second grade. What help he's getting now is too little, too late.

And Tony doesn't know that there will be few if any adjustments in the classroom reading process as a result of his failure—or the failure of five other children in his class—who read at least a year below their grade level. Teachers will do the best they know how to address Tony's needs. But their techniques are aimed at children with Mindy's background, and sometimes there's too much focus on approach and too little focus on whether it works for the child in front of them. They hope that Tony will "develop" into a

---

[2] Quick and reliable assessments of phonemic awareness include the Test of Phonemic Awareness (TOPA), Roswell-Chall, Yopp-Singer, and Rosner.

good reader in time. After all, there are remedial reading classes and special education services for Tony. There is no accountability for not finding methods to address Tony's needs.

> The elegance or political persuasiveness of an educational theory means nothing to a child for whom it does not work.

What Tony does know is that he is dumb. Dumb at science. Dumb at math. Dumb at social studies. He gets the same message every day from every class.[3]

Actually, Tony is a bright kid. He has already figured out that there is not a lot of correlation between working hard and doing well. When a child doesn't read, there is virtually none.

So Tony is reading at a first-grade level and Mindy is reading at an eighth-grade level. And few talk about the eight-year spread because few are aware of it. Some national testing companies truncate the scores and report that Tony and those other five children in his class are reading at second grade-sixth month.

Tony's parents would be devastated to know that he cannot read. They are only moderately concerned when they are told that he is a little behind but will catch up. They remember being a little behind, too.

But Tony's teachers are concerned. They know he literally is not reading. And they accurately predict—as most elementary teachers can—that Tony probably won't make it through high school.

LATER

For Mindy, dozens of doors are already opening. Now, and into middle school/junior high, there are spelling bees, young writer contests, science fairs, history fairs, field trips where she will read labels next to paintings and instructions for interactive exhibits, class and student body offices for which she will make speeches, accelerated and enrichment programs, band, and chorus.

These doors remain closed for Tony. Not only is he way behind in reading, but the sixth-grade curriculum does not deal with letters, sounds, and word attack skills. It is about nouns, verbs, topic sentences, and voice.

Gradually Tony finds ways to resist—ways to cut a class, to miss a day or two or three of school. What does it really matter? He becomes more comfortable with those like him—those who belittle teachers, assignments, and

---

[3] K. E. Stanovich, "Matthew Effects in Reading: Some Consequences of Individual Differences in the Acquisition of Literacy," *Reading Research Quarterly* 21 (1986): 360-407.

Table 2
Office Referrals for Disciplinary Infractions by Reading Level
Highlands Middle School Sixth Grade, Kennewick, Washington, 1997-98

	STUDENTS		REFERRALS	
	No.	%	No.	%
Students Reading				
At/above grade level	176	72%	108	37%
Below grade level	70	28%	183	63%
Totals	246	100%	291	100%
Above Grade Level: Numbers of office referrals for discipline infractions				
10+	0	—	0	—
4-10	8	3%	50	17%
3	5	2%	15	5%
2	9	4%	18	6%
1	25	10%	25	9%
0	129	53%	0	0%
Subtotal	176	71%	108	37%
Below Grade Level: Numbers of office referrals for discipline infractions				
10+	6	2%	79	27%
4-10	10	4%	69	24%
3	3	1%	9	3%
2	5	2%	10	3%
1	16	7%	16	6%
0	30	12%	0	0%
Subtotal	76	28%	183	63%

Seven percent of sixth graders, all reading below grade level, accounted for 54% of all office referrals for disciplinary infractions. Fourteen percent of seventh graders (not shown in Table 2) reading below grade level accounted for 57% of all office referrals for disciplinary infractions.

homework, and who call those who excel "nerds." He figures he's not getting it anyway, so why not break his pencil, turn his math homework into paper airplanes, try out that round white pill, flaunt some gang insignia, and hang out where he feels a little better? The principal's office is not so bad, really. He has been there five times already. Mindy hasn't been there once.

MUCH LATER

By high school, Mindy is still on cruise control. She still reads four to five grades above grade level, is involved in student government, plays sports, writes for the school paper, sings in chorale, and has practiced taking the SAT since eighth grade. She can't imagine not going to college.

Tony, on the other hand, is reading at a sixth-grade level. He's sitting in heterogeneous-grouped classes and getting slaughtered. He failed two classes first semester and is flunking another one in his second semester. He suddenly realizes that he is not getting moved along automatically from grade to grade. He isn't getting credit for high school classes he fails. His counselor tells him that he won't graduate in four years if he doesn't buckle down. He is panicked and despairing. He really hits the books after that, but he can't cut it. In numerical terms, Tony has read about 800,000 words in his lifetime outside school. Mindy has read about 14 million.[4]

> "We never really leave our nonreading children behind. We may forget about them, but we are chained to them socially and economically. Like a ship and its anchor, we must either lift them or drag them along behind us."
>
> —Lynn Fielding, Kennewick School Board

The competitive difference seems to surface everywhere except P.E. and metal shop. "I'm good with my hands," Tony tells himself. "I'm sixteen. I'm outta here."

But Tony has low skills. Low employment skills generally pay minimum wage if they pay at all. And Tony lacks the reading ability to qualify for any apprenticeship programs. His friends suggest a little shoplifting, a few random purse snatchings, and the occasional daytime home theft to help out. Tony's going for it. It is one of the few doors that has opened for him.

IT'S NOW AGAIN

By the time Mindy is graduating from a four-year college, Tony has drifted in and out of a dozen jobs and a couple of jails. He has a couple of really cute kids from different relationships. Of course, he does not read to his children. There are lots of reasons—time, distance, money, and the fact that Tony himself reads poorly. So these cute kids will go to kindergarten with forty or fifty hours of pre-literacy experiences. They are not ready to read. At kindergarten they meet their own Mindys who have a thousand hours of pre-literacy experience—and the cycle starts again.

---

[4] At the fifth grade, children at the 90th percentile read 2,357,000 words per year from newspapers, magazines, and books versus 134,000 words per years for those at the 20th percentile. Anderson, Wilson, and Fielding, "Growth in Reading and How Children Spend Their Time Outside of School," *Reading Research Quarterly* 23 (1988): 285-303. Those numbers have been multiplied by six, assuming that this relationship holds true from fourth grade through ninth grade. Mindy's total is derived by multiplying 2,357,000 words per year by six years and Tony's by multiplying 134,000 words per year by six years.

AND SO WE CONCLUDE

Add up other disadvantages for all of the other Tonys. What if some, or even most, of their language experiences are not in English? What if they can't sleep at night because someone is screaming in the next room, or worse? What if they have only one parent only part of the time? What if there is not a clean, quiet place to do homework, or never a safe place to put it after it is finished? What if there isn't a dad or an older sister to help with a science project? What if no one ever goes to parent-teacher conferences?

All of these problems will make it harder to overcome Tony's nonreading handicap. They may make it impossible. Yet the real handicap is still that Tony cannot read.

If a child cannot read, she or he bears the consequences mostly alone—embarrassment now, intensifying frustration with each school year, and later an adulthood of limited options. We all know someone who struggles, sometimes in open frustration, sometimes in silent shame, with illiteracy. It may be a fifth-grader who refuses to bring her schoolbooks home

The Face of Crime

- *One out of every 193 Americans is incarcerated.[5]*
- *49% of them read at or below a ninth-grade level.[6]*

The annual cost of arresting, trying, and imprisoning those whom we did not teach to read in the first, second, and third grades is approximately the same amount we annually spend nationwide educating our 36.7 million K-8 public school students.[7]

to complete her assignments. It may be an uncle who always asks "the wife" to read the newspaper headlines aloud. It may be the teenager on the camping trip who wads up the song sheet and throws it in the fire, declaring, "This is stupid." The fact is that 26% of adults in America age sixteen or older today cannot read well enough to review a pay stub and write down

---

[5] *A Fine Line: Losing American Youth to Violence*—A Special Report of the Charles Stewart Mott Foundation (Flint, MI: Mott Foundation, 1994);

[6] Washington State Department of Corrections, scores from Tests of Adult Basic Education Survey, 1997, in authors' possession.

[7] The annual cost of crime is $425 billion. This sum does not include health care costs for injury, property damage, or losses from injury or death. "Economics of Crime," *Businessweek*, Dec. 13, 1993, 72. Crimes committed by those reading significantly below grade level cost $208 billion annually ($425 billion x 49%). The cost of K-8 public education was approximately $201.4 billion in 1994-95 (calculated by multiplying the total elementary and secondary public school expenditures of $279 billion by 72%–32.3 million K-8 students are 72% of the 44.8 million K-12 students in public schools). Thomas D. Snyder, Charlene M. Hoffman, and Claire M. Geddes, *Digest of Education Statistics* 1997 (Washington, DC: U.S. Department of Education, National Center for Education Statistics, 1997), 11, 36.

the year-to-date gross pay or write a letter about an error that appears on a credit card bill.[8]

Haven't we all wondered how there can be a 20% adult illiteracy rate without a 20% third-grade illiteracy rate? They can't all be recent immigrants.

The usual solution is to blame our teachers. That is an exercise in wrong-headed futility. Nobody has a higher stake than teachers have in teaching children to read. If teachers alone could solve the problem, they would have solved it long ago.

The second most common solution is to spend more money. But if money could buy a literate society, we would have bought one already.

How can we teach our Tonys to read? We need to create an accountability system to assure that it happens.

Productivity Losses from Illiteracy

A 1988 study of eight Southeastern states by the U.S. Department of Labor's regional office in Atlanta concludes, "Conservatively, adult literacy problems are already costing the Southeast regional economy $57.2 billion annually or $4,737 per adult illiterate. This estimated annual cost amounts to 1/5th of the region's total business earnings in 1985."[9]

---

[8] *Data Volume for the National Education Goals Report*, Vol. 1 (Washington, DC: U.S. Government Printing Office, 1995), 121.

[9] Qtd. in MDC, Inc., *Meeting the Economic Challenge of the 1990's: Workforce Literacy in the South* (Chapel Hill, NC: MDC/Sunbelt Institute, 1998), 14-15. If this loss is extrapolated across the United States on the basis of population—and then cut by a third just to be conservative—those costs are $251 billion annually. Others calculate that 75% of the unemployed and 33% of mothers receiving Aid to Families with Dependent Children read significantly below grade level. Orton Dyslexia Society, "Some Facts about Illiteracy in America," qtd. in J. W. Lerner,"Theories for Intervention in Reading," in *Reading and the Special Learner*, edited by C. N. Hedley and J. S. Hicks (Norwood, NJ: Ablex Publishing, 1988), 11.

CHAPTER FIVE

FIVE STEPS TO READING ACCOUNTABILITY

"There are thousands hacking at the branches of evil to one who is striking at the roots."

—Thoreau

Despite the fact that we as a nation currently spend $75 billion per year on K-3 education and have spent similar amounts for the last fifty years without solving the reading problem, the reading problem can be solved. School board members and superintendents can solve it. Legislators and publishers can assure it. Parental assistance is vital.

In Kennewick, we are getting there. We are not at 90%, but we are getting closer.

For most of the three decades since the 1960s, our scores in elementary reading floated between the 49th and 55th percentile. In May 1995, approximately 55% of our third graders were reading at or above grade level.

In May 1998, 71% of third graders in the Kennewick School District were reading at or above grade level. Two elementary buildings scored above 90%. Three other schools were bobbing in the high seventies and low eighties. Instead of having 25% of our children entering fourth grade reading at a first- and second-grade level, only 15% read at those levels. The rest were reading within five months of the standard.

Think of it: 71%. That's a lot of Tonys who are going to have Mindy results.

Fig. 5.1
Percentage of Third Grade Students Reading at Grade Level
Fall and Spring, Kennewick, 1995 - 1998

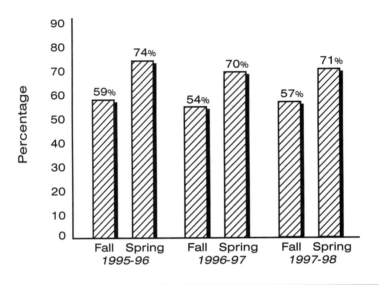

Kennewick is an ordinary school district with an ordinary budget. It has a school board made up of hard-working but ordinary citizens, a fine superintendent, solid principals, dedicated teachers, an active union, and a supportive community. It's probably a lot like your school district and community.

Our scores are going to continue to improve, too. We have created accountability for reading in our schools and in our homes. We believe we understand what happened, and how you can replicate the process with these results in your school district, community, and state.

What We Did: Five Things

We believe that the five most important things that we did were:

1. The board set a clear, measurable goal in the spring of 1995: 90% of third graders will read at or above grade level by the spring of 1998. The goal created a line of sight from where each school was to where each school needed to go, within an allotted time frame. The goal became the number one priority of the board and the district, and the number one use of board meeting time. (See Chapter 10.)

2. We established a solid, accurate system for measuring reading ability. This system should extend from kindergarten through grade three. (See Chapters 6 and 11.)

3. We reported the percentage of students reading at or above the standard in grade-level equivalents (see Chapter 12) to three audiences:

> *"Based on our last twenty years' experience, the chance that we could increase the percentage of our third graders reading at grade level to 70% (to say nothing of 90%) without the goal was zero. The goal realigns resources and priorities."*
>
> —Bev Henderson, Assessment/Staff Development Coordinator, Kennewick School District

- Our percentage as a district to the public and to the media
- The percentage of each elementary school to the public, our principals, and our teachers
- The status of each individual student to parents in parent-teacher conferences

4. We issued a district-wide position paper specifically identifying the new and expanded ground rules for reaching the reading goal. (See Chapter 13 about Kennewick's "Reading White Paper.") Key concepts included:

- We measured and reported progress by each elementary building.
- We expected each building to develop its plan to meet this goal.
- We expected three to four years of planned, incremental, and continuous improvement from each individual school's baseline to the goal. We did not expect change overnight.
- We expected each school principal to be accountable for providing leadership for reading growth.
- We expected each school to reallocate its existing resources significantly to focus on the goal. Examples of reallocation included more classroom time spent on reading, more staff training funds spent on reading, and reassignment of teacher assistants. The board would help on the district level.
- We expected excellent early reading instruction. We expected intervention in kindergarten, first, second, and third grades instead of remediation in grades four and five.[1]

---

[1] "The likelihood that a child would be a good or poor reader by the end of fourth grade was almost wholly predicted by whether she or he was a good or poor reader at the end of first grade." Marilyn Jager Adams, Rebecca Treiman, and Michael Pressley, "Reading, Writing, and Literacy," in *Handbook of Child Psychology*. Vol. 4: *Child Psychology in Practice*, edited by William Damon (New York: John Wiley & Sons, 1997), 283.

• District staff did not adopt a singular approach or curriculum— phonics, whole language, or otherwise. The district staff supported any school program reasonably calculated to achieve the goal.

> *Kathy Blasdel's family had been busy all morning with Saturday yard work, laundry, house cleaning, and packing a picnic so they could spend the afternoon at the river on their ski boat. When the jobs were done, Kathy said, "We can go now! Everybody go get your swimsuits on!"*
>
> *Her eight-year-old cried, "We can't go yet. We haven't read for twenty minutes."*
>
> *Kathy reflected, "I don't know what's going on nationwide, but I can tell you that everyone around here knows that you read twenty minutes a day with your children."*
>
> —Kathy Blasdel, Kennewick, Washington

• We expected 90% of our students, regardless of socioeconomic background, to reach the goal.

5. We involved parents, encouraging them to read twenty minutes a day with their child from birth through grade school. We collaborated with citizens to organize a nonprofit corporation called the Reading Foundation. With seed money of one dollar per student, contributed from six of our local districts (now ten of them), this foundation launched a series of low-cost, high-impact activities that began creating a strong cultural expectation that parents read aloud daily with their child. (See Chapters 8, 9, and 14.) It has already had astonishing success.

Why It Worked: Five Reasons

School districts and states can reproduce these five steps. These steps make permanent, self-sustaining change for five reasons.

1. The political leaders who are most responsive to their electorate set the reading goal. These leaders are separate from the educational leaders who are more focused on the issue of how to achieve the goal. Legislators, who provide primary funding to local school districts, are within their legislative function in requiring a process of improvement. Local school boards are within their policy and oversight functions in setting specific levels of measurable minimum skills in reading to be achieved by third and fourth grade. The use of political leadership assures that the reading goal can be set and that it will be set high. It also assures that the goal, if not set at a local level, can be set at a state or national level.

2. The goal is a subtle shift from process to measurable achievement. It is a move from rhetoric to reality. We say that all children can learn. We must now teach 90% of them the basic skill for learning. By establishing a reading goal, the teaching process now has a feedback mechanism that links expectation to results. The goal, its expectations, and the reporting requirements introduce immense institutional pressures to improve from the current baseline. It

    Current and converging research shows that 90% of children with excellent initial instruction, testing, and appropriate intervention beginning in kindergarten can read at grade level by third grade. The problem is not with the current state of research. It is political. Unless we increase the current rates of change, it may take twenty years to implement existing reading research in our elementary schools.

    makes elementary staff concentrate relentlessly on upgrading reading instructional processes—changing, experimenting, evaluating, focusing on what works—for kindergarten through third grade until 90% of their students can read well. It also provides teachers with a powerful justification to eliminate less important curriculum.

3. The goal and reporting mechanisms clarify the mutual dependence between schools and newspapers. The future readership of newspapers depends on children learning to read early and well. Reciprocally, 12% to 30% of our districts' annual operating budget depends on editorial support to pass our levies. The economic relationship between successful schools and successful newspapers has never been more obvious.

4. The goal virtually obliges schools to support parents as their child's first and most important teacher. True, schools may choose to go it alone and accept sole responsibility for teaching reading, but most schools quickly realize that the few dollars needed to train and support parents in reading aloud to their children daily from birth will bring well-prepared kindergartners through school doors each September. Most schools can easily see how the time and energy invested in continuing that encouragement right through elementary school results in thousands of hours of home-volunteer reading. The relationship between supportive schools and engaged parents has never been more evident or necessary.

Newspaper Advertising Revenue Loss
Predicted from Third- and
Fourth-Grade Reading Levels

Number of entering fourth graders per each
100 students who read at first- and second-grade levels .... 25[1]

Number of fourth graders per each
100 students who can be predicted to drop out of
high school based on third-grade data including
reading scores and GPA .... 17.5[2]

Number of these drop-outs who will not
subscribe to newspapers .... 10.5[3]

Annual newspaper advertising revenue
loss per nonsubscriber .... $683.91[4]

Lifetime newspaper advertising revenue
loss per nonsubscriber .... $37,065.00[5]

Lifetime advertising revenue loss to local
newspapers per each 100 students where 25%
enter fourth grade reading at a first- or
second-grade level .... $389,182.50[6]

[1] See Chapter 3.

[2] Seventy percent of later high school drop-outs can be predicted based on reading ability, GPA, IQ, and retention at third grade. Dee Norman Lloyd, "Prediction of School Failure from Third-Grade Data," *Educational and Psychological Measurement* 38 (1978): 1193-1200. The national dropout rate of 25 students per hundred (coincidentally similar to the numbers of fourth graders reading significantly below grade level) x 70% = 17.75.

[3] 60% of those with less than a high school diploma or equivalent do not subscribe to newspapers. (60% x 17.5 = 10.5) Newspaper Association of America *Facts about Newspapers 1997* (1997) 5.

[4] The annual newspaper advertising revenue per each additional subscriber is $683.91, computed by dividing the annual newspaper advertising revenue of $38,402 million by the 56.93 million newspapers subscribers ($38,402 million divided by 56.92 million subscribers = $683.91 per subscriber). See *Advertising Age*, May 12, 1997, for estimated annual advertising revenues and *1997 Editor & Publisher Yearbook* for newspaper subscription estimates. Actual revenues of each local newspaper will vary.

[5] Average age at first subscription is assumed to be twenty-five. Average life expectancy is seventy-five years. Advertising losses from a nonsubscribing nonreader would therefore be incurred for 50 years. The lifetime advertising loss is $37,065, calculated as follows: $683.91 x 50 years = $37,065. The present value of the loss of this lifetime revenue stream can be calculated as well. If the revenue stream is discounted at 5% for the twelve years until the student is twenty-five and if thereafter the discount factor is assumed to approximate annual increases in advertising revenue, the present value of the advertising losses from a lifetime nonsubscriber is approximately $20,639.18.

[6] Lifetime newspaper advertising revenue loss for the 10.5 students whose dropping out of high school can be predicted primarily from their third grade verbal and reading levels and will not subscribe to newspapers is $389,182.50 ($37,065 x 10.5 students = $389,182.50. Additional lost revenue from lost subscriptions has not been included because it has been assumed to approximate the additional production and delivery costs of the newspaper.

As I entered Diane Barber's child development class at Kennewick High, she gestured to a group of students gathered around a girl in her midteens holding her newborn daughter. "This is something you might like to see," she whispered.

The girl's friends were admiring the baby and asking questions such as "How much does she weigh?" and "How was the delivery?"

When there was a pause, I offered my compliments and added, "I hope you're reading to her?"

"Of course! Every night." responded the new mother swiftly. "Her father and I even read to her before she was born."

Stunned at the image of two unwed teens reading to their unborn child, I managed to ask, "How did you know to do that?"

Before she could answer, another teen jumped in, "Twenty minutes a day! It's everywhere—radio, TV, newspapers. You've got to read to children."

—Nancy Kerr, President, the Reading Foundation

5. The goal creates pre-funded, self-sustaining accountability among the adults in four of our five major institutions—the schools, the home, the press (and, by extension, the economic sector of society) and the legislature (government). The schools already receive about $500,000 for each class of twenty-five students from kindergarten through third grade.[2] The essential school funding issue is to redirect this money. Homes, newspapers, and the state each have a continuing economic interest in increasing reading skills. Once the reading goal, tests, and reporting mechanisms are in place, it is nearly impossible to eliminate them. Each institution quickly tilts toward cooperation in achieving the goal. Reporting the annual results of the reading goal, school progress, or school decline is news. And help from millions of parents is there for the asking.

These five simple steps are within the power of every school board and superintendent. Once taken, these steps become permanent, self-sustaining, system-wide changes.

---

[2] $6,000 times 25 children per class=$150,000 per year times 3.5 years = $525,000.

CHAPTER SIX

TWENTY QUESTIONS

"A four-fold thrust for leadership by local school boards will ensure excellence . . .Vision, Structure, Accountability, and Advocacy."

—National School Board Association[1]

Question 1. In simple terms, what is Kennewick's third-grade reading accountability mechanism?

It is the annual measuring and reporting of progress toward the district's reading goal (90% of third-graders reading at or above grade level within three years) on a building-by-building basis.

Question 2. Why have a goal?

Kennewick's reading accountability focuses on an output (specified numbers of students reading at specified standards) instead of inputs (more teachers or a specified curriculum). This focus on output is a paradigm shift from public education's traditional focus on input/process. One approach for reaching the goal is to increase the money (increase the inputs) we spend K-3. However,

> *"The 90% reading goal makes us focus on those reading below grade level. It makes us focus on the struggling reader."*
>
> —John Hodge,
> Kennewick School Board

---

[1] National School Board Association, Article II of Beliefs and Policies, Constitution and Bylaws, 9-10, adopted by the Delegate Assembly, April 25 and 28, 1997, Anaheim, CA.

READING ACCOUNTABILITY: What It Is

Reading accountability is a high-level district or state policy creating a minimum but high elementary reading standard, an institutional commitment that most students' reading performance reach the reading standard, a testing and reporting system, and the shifting of organizational priorities and resources at appropriate levels to achieve the growth.

Like other policy changes, reading accountability is visible in changed adult expectations, in the increased flow and enhanced importance of certain information, and in the adult responses required by that information. It is most visible in:

- Administrator and staff discussions about the difference between current reading levels and the reading goal in their jurisdiction
- The increased importance of the initial reading baseline, subsequent testing, amount of growth, and reporting
- The reallocation of personnel and resources toward elementary reading
- The analysis of reading improvement by classroom in elementary meetings
- The creation of teaching teams and articulated curricula
- Staff decisions to eliminate less effective instructional techniques
- Parents' involvement in reading
- Sustained community interest, including regular media reports
- Regular monitoring of student progress toward the goal

READING ACCOUNTABILITY: What It's Not

Reading accountability is not an instructional program. When we visit a classroom, what we see are segments of instructional programs. We do not see reading accountability which is invisible to a casual classroom observer. In a classroom we might see:

- Phoneme screening tests
- Small reading groups
- Explicit phonics
- Rhyming charts
- Blending exercises
- Story-telling and story-reading
- Big Books
- Reading journals
- Predicting
- Embedded phonics
- Cross-age tutoring

These different reading practices, specialized teaching techniques, and curriculum are synthesized into thousands of classroom instructional approaches, none of which is reading accountability. Reading accountability is a board or state policy that creates a system change. The system change is the primary result. The curriculum change resulting from it is secondary.

there seems to be little correlation between increased funding and increased student achievement. Kennewick's approach is to state the desired student outcome, give educators the freedom to reallocate existing resources to reach that goal, and hold them accountable for doing so.

Question 3. What instructional programs do you recommend?

None. The district prescribes no instructional programs or procedures. It makes no text or curriculum recommendations. Instructional program selection is specifically left to school professionals.

> *"Neither Congress or any state legislature nor any federal or state agency should establish a national or state reading methodology."*
>
> –Ken Goodman[2]

There are proven practices with a high probability of success, and there are common elements or criteria that all good instructional programs should have at appropriate age levels. While a school can use any combination of instructional approaches to reading, ineffective ones get weeded out rather quickly. Principals and teachers are highly motivated to seek out optimal programs as they become more accountable for those choices.

Third-grade reading accountability functions like a scale in weight loss programs or like a stopwatch in track events. It is a measurement instrument of different instructional programs. It is not an instructional program. It measures the effectiveness of each building's reading program for the students in that building. Baselining and measuring growth building by building minimizes an initial higher or lower starting point.

> *"The key to reading accountability is a consistent goal measured with the same tool across the district. The measure gives teachers, parents, students, and administrators good objective data, often for the first time, for effective decision making."*
>
> —Paul Rosier
> Superintendent, Kennewick School District

Question 4. How effective is this accountability approach?

Over the last three years, each of our thirteen elementary schools increased the percentage of its third graders reading at or above grade level by at least 6%. Some increased by as much as 28%. Virtually all of that growth has been retained in fourth and fifth grade as these children are progressing through the system. (See Appendix D,

---

[2]Ken Goodman, *In Defense of Good Teaching: What Teachers Need to Know about the Reading Wars* (York, ME: Stenhouse, 1998), 34.

The Northwest Evaluation Association

15115 S.W. Sequoia Parkway, Suite 200
Portland, Oregon 97224
Phone: (503) 624-1951
Fax: (503) 639-7873
http://www.nwea.org

The Northwest Evaluation Association (NWEA) is an educational nonprofit organization currently serving over 200,000 students in 150 school districts in twenty-one states.

The NWEA provides:

- Data banks of weighted and nationally normed questions
- Software for district test creation
- Initial scoring and interpretation
- Staff training and support

The NWEA test banks and software allow each district to create a series of overlapping tests, each of which measures reading ability over a portion of the grades 2-10 continuum. See Chapter 11 for additional information.

Success for All

Robert Slavin, Johns Hopkins University
3003 N. Charles Street
Baltimore, MD 21218
Phone: (800) 548-4998/(410) 516-8809
Fax: (410) 516-8890
http://www.successforall.com

Success for All provides high-quality instruction for students from prekindergarten through sixth grade, tutoring for those struggling in first grade, strong family support systems, and staff training for teachers. It operates programs in 150 of our nation's largest districts, the greatest majority in Title I schools. Start-up costs average $65,000 the first year and $25,000 the second year. These costs are often paid by Title I funds. Success for All requires at least 80% staff approval by secret ballot as a condition of working with an elementary school. Its programs are carefully monitored and are results oriented.

"Retention of Reading Progress As Measured by Percentage of Kennewick Fourth and Fifth Graders Meeting the District Reading Standard.")

Question 5. How is this plan different from what you were doing before?

We were doing plenty of good things before, but our plan began with creating a hierarchy of priorities. First, as a board, we decided that the "academic agenda" was more important than our social

> "In the American public schools, we have four agendas: the athletic agenda, the social agenda, the academic agenda, and the 'keep the ship afloat' agenda. Many districts should clarify that their first and primary commitment is to the academic agenda."
>
> —Dr. Willard Daggett[3]

agenda, our athletic agenda, and our adult employee agenda. We then decided that the first academic priority was to uniformly achieve grade-level reading in K-3.

Second, we changed our focus from process to results by buying the Northwest Evaluation Association test banks. We had been teaching children to read for years, but there simply hadn't been much change in the number of children each year who were actually learning to read. We discovered that it was possible to go through the motions beautifully without ever producing the necessary improvement in many children's reading level. Teachers' job descriptions had formerly stated: "Do X, Y, and Z to teach reading." Now their job descriptions read, "Make it happen by third grade. Make it happen for 90% of your students. How you do it is up to you."

Third, we realized that implicit in the focus on results was consequences. If we as board members, superintendents, or building principals cannot or will not create the teams and systems to deliver our most basic academic skill, we should have the grace to step aside for those who can. Our intermediate step was to report progress by student to parents, and by schools and the district to the public.

Fourth: We gave schools permission to change—to cut other curriculum, to use personnel differently, to bring varying approaches to the classroom, to create a seamless delivery system between the grades. The selection of CORE (Consortium on Reading Excellence) by eight schools and First Steps (an Australian reading model) by five schools for K-5 staff training is an example of that change.

---

[3] Dr. Willard Daggett, President, International Center for Leadership in Education, and educational consultant, 219 Liberty Street, Schenectady, NY 12305, Phone: (518) 377-6878, Fax: (518) 372-7544

CORE
Consortium for Reading Excellence

5500 Shellmound Street, Suite 140
Emeryville, CA 94608-2402
Phone: (510) 595-3400
Fax: (510) 595-3434
e-mail: Lindad@coreread.com

Consortium for Reading Excellence (CORE) was created by Linda Diamond and Bill Honig, California's former Superintendent of Public Instruction. By the end of 1998-99 CORE will have trained over 10,000 teachers at more than 300 schools in 40 districts. Literacy First is an affiliated program.

CORE provides six days of in-service training for K-5 teachers in reading research and best instructional practices. Training is followed by classroom visits for coaching and demonstrations. CORE provides a binder detailing the classroom level techniques and testing needed in:

- Phonological awareness
- Spelling
- Vocabulary
- Phonics
- Comprehension
- Implementation

Their pivotal research indicates that if the processes are consistently applied commencing in kindergarten, 85%-90% of most school populations can read at or above grade level by the end of third grade.

First Steps

Heinemann/First Steps/Reading Recovery
361 Hanover Street
Portsmouth, NH 03801
Phone: (800) 541-2086/(603 431-7894

First Steps is a literacy resource developed by the Western Australian Department of Education and currently implemented in 200 districts. First Steps is based on instructional practices that teachers have identified as effective. Student skills are measured along developmental continua for each model with embedded phonic instruction. Modules include oral language development, writing, reading, and spelling. First Steps provides two days of teaching in each model for each teacher with the option of tutor training. The ten days of intensive training allow districts to develop their own trainers.

Fifth, thinking "outside the box" is now our norm. We needed to change our community's awareness, so that parents would enthusiastically support this reading program. We facilitated the organization of a 501(c)(3) nonprofit corporation, the Reading Foundation, to do it. The discussion has shifted away from how we always did it in the past to what we must do differently in the future to achieve the goal.

Question 6. Why third grade? Why not earlier or later?

From kindergarten through the third grade, children need to learn to read well and independently because, from the third grade onward, children use their reading skills to learn in specific content areas. The second and third grades mark the transition from acquiring the skill to using the skill. In K-3, children learn to read. From 3-12, they read to learn.

Question 7. Don't most of our children already read at grade level?

No. (See Chapter 3.) By the beginning of third grade, children read on eight different grade levels, ranging from nonreaders through the eighth-grade level. We now understand that, when about 40% of our fourth graders nationally can't read fourth-grade material, it simply means this: When those students started third grade a year earlier, about 13% of them were reading at a kindergarten level, about 14% were reading at a first-grade level, and about 16% were reading at a second-grade level.

When we look at grade-level equivalents at fourth grade for national tests, we need to realize that many of these tests truncate the scores somewhere around second grade/sixth month. What are the results? We get our poorest management information about the student's most important skill at its most critical time period.

Question 8. Don't our remediation programs catch up the students who are behind?

Remediation is very expensive and ineffective. Seventy percent of those students who presently are not reading at grade level by the end of the third grade will never read at grade level.

Question 9. Why should we focus on reading and not math or science?

All of the "basics" are not equal. The foundation of the academic basics is reading. Reading is the skill necessary to access the curriculum in books, on blackboards, and in computers. Students who read significantly below grade level are like lumberjacks with dull saws—they work harder and achieve less. The first thing they should do is sharpen their saws.

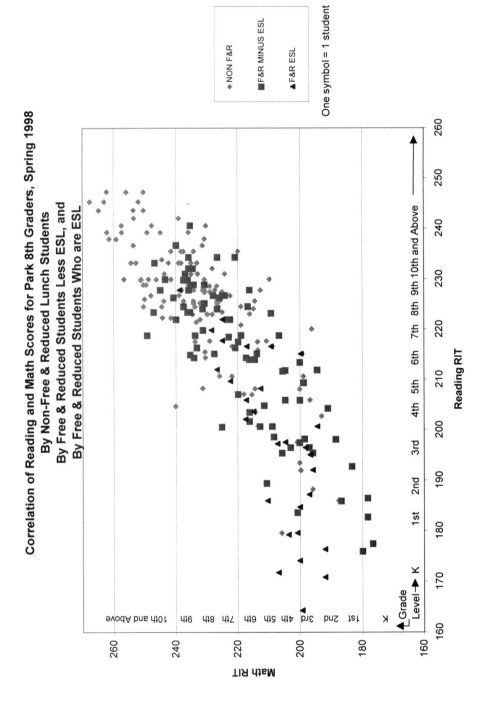

Correlation of Reading and Math Scores for Park 8th Graders, Spring 1998
By Non-Free & Reduced Lunch Students
By Free & Reduced Students Less ESL, and
By Free & Reduced Students Who are ESL

NON F&R
F&R MINUS ESL
F&R ESL

One symbol = 1 student

Reading RIT

Math RIT

Children who cannot read will do poorly in math and science. They cannot decipher story problems. They cannot understand the linkages of cause and effect that underlie scientific processes. In short, they cannot read and understand the math textbooks and the science textbooks. Spending time to teach children to read will, in the long run, teach them more math and science than spending more time on math and science will teach them. Students who read well do better in every academic subject because every academic subject requires reading.

> *"40% of the errors on math achievement tests are reading errors."*
>
> —Mary Lee Barton; "Addressing the Literacy Crisis: Teaching Reading in the Content Area," *Bulletin* (McRel), March 1997, 22-30.

Question 10: Why should we target only 90% to read at grade level? Why not target all students?

About 12% of school-aged students require special education. Through developmental delays or physical, mental, and/or emotional handicaps, about half of these children are not capable of reading at the same grade level as their peers. About 6-7% of this 12%, while disabled in some areas, can still be good readers. This leaves 5% of special education children who cannot reach the goal. Perhaps another 4-5% of our students who are not classified as special-needs children have social and emotional issues, are extremely transient, and/or are non-English monolingual and won't achieve the goal. Setting our sights on 90% reaches most of the reachable readers.

Question 11: Is 90% really achievable? Are we just setting ourselves up to fail?

It depends on how we define failure. Has Kennewick failed because, after three years, our district average is 71%? Possibly, but we don't think so. We did not reach 90% as a district within three years. but some of our buildings reached it, and others are in the 80% range.

Declaring the goal involves significant risks, foremost among them failure. For educators who have spent their professional lives working by the old seat-time paradigm, this goal will feel impossible. We think 90% is stretching the system, but that it is achievable.

First-year gains come because third-grade teachers spend more time on reading. Second-year gains come because the K-2 teachers coordinate their programs more closely. However, unless kindergarten, first-, and second-grade teachers immediately reallocate time, energy, and resources during the first year of the goal, each of those classes will move into the next grade with approximately the same number of children reading below grade level.

Unless second-grade teachers engage the first year of the goal, second graders will enter the third grade at about the same level as the prior class. Third-grade teachers will then work just as hard the second year of the goal with the same percentage gain in children reading at grade level. Third- and fourth-year gains will come as K-3 teachers replace curriculum which does not work for their students.

The job of reaching the 90% goal becomes easier to achieve in every classroom as parents make a habit of reading twenty minutes a day with their children at home from birth through elementary school so that every child enters school from a literacy-rich environment. Long-term gains will come when we create an expectation of parental accountability.

Question 12. Why did you target "continual improvement" over a certain time period?

We expect each elementary school to make annual and continuous improvement. We expect improvement in kindergarten and first grade, even though it will not be evident on the third-grade test until two or three years later. We expect that kindergarten and first-grade improvement will be built upon by second- and third-grade teachers.

Continual improvement has other dimensions. In every district, some elementary schools will have much further to go than others. In addition, incremental improvement becomes more difficult as a school approaches the 90% goal. The last 5% growth is more difficult than the first 5% growth. The first 5% growth moves the students already very close to grade level up to the standard. The last 5% growth must move students who would normally be two years below grade level up to the standard.

Question 13. Why did you choose a certain time period?

A definite time period creates a reality check and motivation. Absent a deadline, the reading goal has secondary institutional importance and is at the mercy of issues that do. Annual reports of expected growth over three or four years create an appropriate sense of urgency.

Question 14. Why report by grade-level equivalents? Why not the statistical averages, means, medians, stanines and percentiles traditionally used by educators?

There are more Americans who speak Greek fluently than Americans who are fluent in statistics. Statistics is a foreign language understood by probably fewer than 2% of board members or educators, and by even fewer parents and legislators.

Reporting in grade-level equivalents provides clear and honest information about how the education system, in general, and how a student, in particular, is doing. What does it mean to parents, board members, and educators that a child is reading at the 30th percentile? Usually not very much. However say, "This third-grader is reading at a first-grade level," and everyone understands that the child is in dire straits and needs help immediately.

Question 15. What about costs?

What drives current student performance levels in schools? Usually it's scheduling personnel, classroom time, curriculum approaches, and sensitivity to results. A significant driver of current student performance levels in homes is time spent reading aloud with children. Change is most likely to occur by changing the drivers. It will not occur if we do not change home patterns, or, within our schools, if we do not reallocate existing personnel, time, resources, or create accountability for results.

In Kennewick we have about $17.5 million in existing resources (3,500 K-3 elementary students x $5,000 = $17.5 million) available to K-3 to be used on this focused goal. We achieved the results of our first year—an

---

The Economics of Reading

The United States currently spends about $75 billion on our K-3 educational delivery system. About 25% of these children enter fourth grade reading at only a first- or second-grade level. Even if it were to cost another $18.2 billion (one-fourth of $75 billion) to teach that lower 25% to read at grade level, we would recover that amount from a reduction in the direct social costs of incarceration, public assistance, public medical care, and public housing that society pays every single year. But we do not have to make this kind of additional investment. We merely have to redirect how a portion of this $75 billion dollars will be used to create literacy accountability.

Setting high-level policies to create the first academic standard in elementary schools and to establish the testing and reporting systems costs comparatively little:

- about $5 per student for testing
- about $1 per student for scoring and reporting

By being candid about the gulf between actual and perceived reading levels, we create the institutional will to reallocate existing resources toward reading and away from other good but less powerful educational objectives.

---

increase from 59% to 74% within the existing budget. In the second year, we used an additional $150,000 that went to staff training and curriculum. The third year we allocated $500,000 from our levy that went to extensive staff training and materials. However, the real leverage did not come from new funds. It came from reallocating existing funds within our schools and from enlisting parents in our homes.

Question 16. Socioeconomic status (SES) is highly correlated with academic performance. We cannot increase the academic performance of children before improving their parents' socioeconomic status, can we?

As board members, we need to distinguish positive correlations from actual causes. During the Depression, most of those who learned to read were poor by today's standards. Our public schools today have many high-achieving students from difficult socioeconomic circumstances and many low-achieving students from excellent socioeconomic circumstances.

Thirty-two percent of students reading below grade level on the National Assessment of Educational Progress (NAEP) had parents who were college graduates.[5] This condition could not occur if socioeconomic status caused low academic performance. What causes a low SES English as a Second Language (ESL) student to achieve higher than high SES students? What causes a high SES student to perform not only lower than low SES students but other high SES students as well? The cause is more subtle than mere socioeconomic status.

Quiz

Are these positive correlations causal?

· *The positive correlation between dietary fat and the incidence of cancer*

· *The positive correlation between shoe size and vocabulary size in children*

The primary difference between the poor who do well in school and the poor who do not do well in school stems from their pre-kindergarten literacy experience. Successful children from low socioeconomic circumstances generally have hundreds of hours of literacy experience, have an extensive spoken vocabulary, and are familiar with sounds,

---

[5] G. Reid Lyon, Ph.D., Chief of the Child Development and Behavior Branch of the National Institute of Child Health and Human Development (NICHD), National Institute of Health (NIH), *Statement before the Committee on Education and the Workforce, U.S. House of Representatives, Washington, D.C. Thursday, July 10, 1997,* 7-21. For the scores of California students whose parents were college graduates, see Dr. Lyon's *Statement before the Committee of Labor and Human Resources, United States Senate, Washington, D.C., Tuesday, April 28, 1998,* reproduced in Appendix B.

words, and books. They come to school ready to learn to read. Unsuccessful children from low socioeconomic circumstance generally have little literacy experience.

The average child in an affluent school comes to kindergarten with a thousand hours of literacy experience. The average child in a nonaffluent school may come with as few as twenty-five hours of literacy experience.[6] Academic performance can be significantly improved by increasing children's pre-kindergarten literacy experience regardless of their socioeconomic status.

Parents Make the Difference

Imagine a kid who practices batting and pitching a ball to his dad an hour every day all summer, from the time the child is three until he is eight. [May, June, July, August = 120 hours a year for 5 years.]

Imagine a second kid—no practice, no training, has never slipped his hand in a baseball glove, has never run the bases, has never swung a bat, has almost never seen a full game played.

Imagine that they turn out the same day for Little League try-outs.

The skill level between these two young ball players is like the skill level in reading readiness of our incoming kindergartners.

Parents who read twenty minutes a day with their children from birth have a kindergartner who has received 608 hours (365 days divided by 3 [20 minutes is one third of an hour] = 121.6 hours a year times 5 years = 608 hours) of literacy experience prior to kindergarten. Parents can do so much more with very little effort—for instance, asking their child to find the "M" at McDonald's and simply asking, "What do you think will happen next?" while telling a story. Our districts will receive valuable benefit at relatively little cost by systematically encouraging parents to read aloud with their children.

It appears that we can increase academic performance in children without changing their low socioeconomic status if we can increase their pre-literacy experience. It is also critical to assure pre-literacy experience for children of moderate to higher socioeconomic status in our communities.

---

[6] Marilyn Jager Adams, *Beginning to Read: Thinking and Learning about Print* (Cambridge, MA: MIT Press, 1990), 89; William H. Teale, "Home Backgrounds and Young Children's Literacy Development," in *Emergent Literacy,* edited by W. H. Teale and E. Sulzby (Norwood, NJ: Ablex Publishing, 1986), 173-206.

Child by Child

When we ask our teachers to tell us the "real story" of how the district program is working in their school, they remind us that it works only child by child.

Steve Linn, an energetic third-grade teacher in Lincoln Elementary, pinpoints three problems with the test-driven goal: First, because of very high turnover rates at some schools, "those tested may not be the product of the system testing them." Second, the testing tells the teacher if the student is reading at grade level, but "not the specific weaknesses a student has in the reading process. We need more information to allow focused and intentional teaching." Third, and perhaps more seriously, the goal itself may send an unintended negative message that progress "doesn't count."

Steve reported one student who entered with a 157 RIT score, 31 points below the expected level of an entering third grader. This girl engaged seriously with reading and improved to a 176 RIT score—"two years plus of growth in a single year, yet according to the district goal of 194, she's a failure. Somehow, we need to reward progress while at the same time asking why so little reading growth occurred for her during the prior two and one-half years."

A sensitive and dedicated third-grade teacher* in Kennewick spoke up strongly for more individualized assessment. One of her twenty-three students during the last twelve months, April to April, was dealing with such family turmoil that "this child can't think about school." It began when the divorced father remarried and wanted the child to live with them two weeks out of every month. The stepmother was a total stranger at the time of the marriage; not only that, within the year, this marriage disintegrated. When she left, she took the child's clothes, toys, and bed with her. Meanwhile, within the same year, the child's twice-married mother, who had had a live-in boyfriend for more than a year, married a third time to a man she had known only briefly.

No wonder this student had one of the "lowest scores of any third grader in our school" on the fall test. Yet amazingly, this child had come up twenty points by January. "I don't think [the student] will make the district goal this spring, but this shows great progress considering what has happened this year," summarized the teacher.

*Teacher is anonymous to protect the identity of the student

Question 17. Why not just retain the third graders who aren't reading well? Why not hold the children accountable?

Few, if any, children do not want to read. At school they are in the right place to learn. In fact, society funds schools because schools promise to teach them to read. Teaching is the job of the adults in the system, and the way to tell if the adults have succeeded in teaching is to determine if the children have succeeded in learning.

> *The subtle allure of the socioeconomic argument for educators is that it places the primary responsibility of poor academic performance on society. The "problem" with the reading-as-the-primary-cause-of-school-failure thesis for educators is that it places the primary responsibility of academic performance on schools.*

Furthermore, we are talking about *children*—ages five, six, seven, and eight. When the problem is defined as the mismatch of program to student need—a decision that adults make—then it's clear that the primary accountability needs to be with the adults.

Yes, some children may need more time. Not all children have equal capacity, equal motivation, and equal support. However, when a child isn't reading, it means that the adult or the adult systems have failed, not that the child has failed. We need to accept that accountability and find ways to deliver literacy. Matching appropriate instructional techniques and amounts of time with the child is an adult problem. It requires an adult solution. Holding adults primarily accountable creates change where it needs to occur.[7]

Question 18. What have been your most significant problems in achieving the goal?

First, we failed to monitor the reading process at kindergarten, first, and second grades as contemplated by our Reading White Paper. Although we were encouraged and impressed by the growth we saw, it

---

[7] Kennewick retains elementary school students fairly infrequently and on a case by case basis, but it has a serious middle school promotion/retention policy. Sixth-, seventh-, and eighth-grade students failing one or more classes are retained based on the number of failed classes, class attendance, and district test scores. Retained students may be promoted by successfully completing an optional summer school at their parents' expense (tuition $165). Beginning in 1995-96, Kennewick started this program for the 3,000 students at its four middle schools. Based on three years of experience, typically 450 students are notified in January of possible retention. Fifty percent engage and meet the standard for promotion; 25% attend summer school with a 90% completion rate. More than half of the sixth- (47%), seventh- (60%), and eighth-(58%) grade students retained read below grade level. This program won a national award for innovation, the 1998 Grand Prize Magna Award and was featured in the *American School Board Journal*, April 1998.

primarily occurred during third grade. When we discovered that second graders at many schools continued to score in the spring at the same levels year after year, we realized that administrators and teachers needed good assessments at kindergarten, first, and second grades as well as at third grade. We have responded by using ongoing diagnostic tests and by measuring students' reading skills from kindergarten through third grade.

> "Our teachers must become more diagnostic and intentional in their teaching. They must have the skills and knowledge to identify and remediate specific reading problems. Specific prescriptive teaching will cause a number of organizational changes within our schools and classrooms. We will improve our student achievement by improving the interactions between teachers and students. Continuous, well-coordinated teacher training is the key."
>
> —Greg Fancher, Director of Elementary Education, Kennewick School District

The second problem is that transient students arrive in our system for fragments of the school year. They often arrive reading below grade level and leave the same way after a few months. We have identified this problem, but we haven't begun to solve it.

The third problem is an inadequate depth of teacher preparation in newly certified teachers and an inadequate depth in current staff training to deal with the reading problems of our lowest 25% of students.

Question 19. How do you deal with principals who don't change?

Principals change. Boards, superintendents, and legislators are creating the first academic system standard that most elementary principals have seen in their entire careers. This standard, no matter what other reservations educators have, organizationally reaffirms one of their strongest beliefs—that children must read to succeed.[8]

We need to give the primary policy and structural changes a little time before we expect the personnel changes to occur. It has taken boards, superintendents, and legislators literally decades to do the job of focusing on student academic achievement and focusing on the structure in which it must occur. It will take principals a few years to focus themselves and each of their schools.

---

[8] Fifty-two percent of elementary teachers identified building basic literacy skills as education's most important goal. The next two were promoting personal growth (23%) and promoting good work habits and discipline (12%). Thomas D. Snyder, Charlene M. Hoffman, and Claire M. Geddes, *Digest of Education Statistics 1997* (Washington, DC: U.S. Department of Education, National Center for Education Statistics, 1997), 31.

Yet the rate of change is nothing short of astonishing, once it takes hold. At virtually all of our Kennewick schools, the rate of curriculum change and focus on student achievement occurred at a speed unmatched at any point during the three preceding decades.

Question 20. Are there any other reasons to establish a district- or a state-wide educational goal?

The best way to pass bonds and levies is to implement the basic findings about public attitudes that have been replicated virtually without change ever since Public Agenda's 1994 *First Things First: What Americans Expect from the Public Schools.*

The first things parents want from their schools are safe campuses and orderly classrooms. Next they want their children taught the basics. The best way to show parents that we are teaching their children the basics is to teach 90% of their children to read at grade level by third grade.

CHAPTER SEVEN

THE KENNEWICK EXPERIENCE

"The task is not so much to see what no one yet has seen, but to think what nobody has yet thought about that which everyone sees."

—Schopenhauer

We share the Kennewick story in hopes that it will smooth the path for you. There will be differences and there will be similarities. The actual process will never be identical from district to district, but many elements will be the same. As common concerns and decisions occur, you can take some comfort in improving this spiralling learning process in your jurisdiction.

Our story began at a meeting in December 1994, when two board members, our superintendent, assistant superintendent, high school director, and a middle school principal met to analyze high school data. The concerns were obvious.

- Why the dramatic leap in D's and F's for the incoming freshman class compared to their eighth-grade year?
- Why were 20% of our high school students dropping out?
- What, precisely, was the seemly obvious connection between dropping out and low GPAs?
- Why was the discipline referral rate of students with a GPA of 2.0 or less five times higher than those with a GPA of 2.1 or higher?
- And why the "glass ceiling" phenomenon? Why did students with a C or lower in English rarely get higher than a C in any other academic subject?

We were slowly honing in on the common thread of a language arts problem in the middle school when Paul Rosier, our superintendent, cleared his throat, and focused the group on the root cause. "Actually, this is a second-grade reading problem," he said. "By and large these are the children who don't learn to read by second grade and never catch up."[1]

We looked again at the data. He was right. The board was still looking at the data in January 1995 when we held a district-wide meeting with K-3 teachers to discuss reading. Teachers filled whiteboards with scores of problems and possible solutions. Administrators listed examples of successes and failures. We collected opinions.

After two hours, a board member suggested: "What we need is a clear goal so we can tell where we are, where we are going, and when we get there. Something like—90% of our second graders will read at grade level in the next three years."

The teachers were stunned: "But that's impossible!"

Then the board was stunned: "Why is it impossible? Aren't we almost there already?"

Dr. Rosier then explained to the board members and staff that such a project had never been achieved in the history of U.S. public education. He told the "Motorola story." His concluding words that evening were, "It's time to think really radically."

In February 1995, the administration formed its District Reading Committee composed of teachers and principals to make recommendations. In May, the district piloted the Northwest Evaluation Association's (NWEA) reading tests, capable of measuring student growth from the beginning to the end of a school year, from third through tenth grades. These tests could be scored in-district in less than a week and the scores could be reported as grade-level equivalents.

In July 1995, the Kennewick Strategic Planning Committee cautiously adopted the reading goal: 90% of our students will read at or above grade level by the end of the third grade by May 1998. We chose third grade rather than second grade as a consensus developed, based on feedback and research, that the second grade was too early. (Appendix C.)

We had an election that fall for four board positions. Two positions were

---

[1] We can identify six or seven out of every ten students who will later drop out from characteristics exhibited in the third grade, primarily reading ability, socioeconomic status, IQ, and retention. It is possible to predict failure almost as accurately in the third grade as the sixth. Norman Lloyd, "Prediction of School Failure from Third Grade Data," *Educational and Psychological Measurement* 38 (1978): 1193-1200.

normally open; the third was open because a member had been appointed to a judgeship, and the fourth was open because a director had moved from the area. All of the winning candidates campaigned on academics in general and the 90% elementary reading goal in particular, from August to October. It was a lively campaign with good media coverage. Parents were interested and gave the winners 65% to 75% approval.

Motorola's Zero Defects Goal

"The problem with education is that you set your goals too low." We were finishing a business/school partnership meeting at Motorola University in Phoenix in 1991. The CEO for the Phoenix division was addressing a group of 75 superintendents. "We used to have that problem at Motorola with defective parts. Virtually every one of our problems led back to defective parts. If we had a dissatisfied customer, it was because their equipment had broken down because of a defective part. Our biggest inventory problem was parts. Repeat sales were hindered by defective parts.

"Every year for ten years, our CEO set a goal to reduce defective parts by 3% to 5%. Some years we got there, some years we didn't. In 1984, during the planning session, our CEO basically said—this problem has plagued us long enough. The goal is to reduce defects by 10 times in the next five years. That meant going from about one defective part in 1,000 to 10,000.

"We were stunned. It was impossible. We could never get there. We mumbled for about three months; but after about three months, we started to see approaches that could get us there— it was just that they were way out of the box—different than anything we had ever done before. One thing built on another. We got there in three years. We set a new goal."

"And what was that?" we asked.

"Six sigma," he said. "About 3.4 part flaws per a million opportunities. We'll be there in a few years. Our biggest problem for years is we were setting our goals too low."

– Paul Rosier, Superintendent, Kennewick School District

The District Reading Committee continued to meet and debate appropriate district-wide instructional strategies. In response to the board member campaigns, increasing community awareness about the goal, and the district reading committee, teachers in the buildings grew increasingly nervous. They recognized the disparity between the high level of verbal commitment by the board and the lack of systemic change in most buildings.

In November 1995, Dr. Rosier and board members met with the District Reading Committee to give some impetus to the stalled initiative. Principals and teachers were concerned about measurable goals and about which instructional model should be imposed across the district. Out of that meeting came "The Kennewick Reading White Paper" (see Chapter 13) in December 1995, which shifted instructional decisions and accountability from the central administration to each elementary principal. The white paper announced, among other things: "An increasing percentage of building principals' annual evaluation will be the result of the leadership principals give to their building toward achieving the reading goal." The principals' response was heated.

A full year had passed. In January 1996, the board announced that it would hold workshops focused on reading with individual elementary schools for the next two years beginning in February. Workshop minutes highlighting innovations and leadership circulated to all elementary teachers, reinforcing the sense of district-wide change. The minutes may have also accelerated change within each building as elementary faculty anticipated showcasing their own school program in the minutes of their own workshop. (See Chapter 13.)

At the first workshop, the board received a thorough exposure to the war between phonetic/whole language approaches.[2] Dr. Rosier and the board concluded that, if the district selected an instructional program or started making decisions about instructional strategies, then principals would be responsible only for implementing those decisions and not for achieving the goal. We chose to decentralize, hold principals accountable for the goal, ride out the turbulence of different programs in different schools, and wait for convergence as successful programs emerged. This proved to be a smart (or very lucky) decision.

In February 1996, we released the final version of the Kennewick Reading White Paper. Included with the white paper was a breakdown of the NWEA Functional Level test by raw scores and grade-level equivalence by each school. (See Appendix C.)

---

[2] See also Appendix F for an overview of whole language, phonics and phonological awareness. See also R. C. Aukerman, *Approaches to Beginning Reading*, 2d ed. (New York: Wiley, 1984); Steven A. Stahl and Bruce A. Murray, "Defining Phonological Awareness and its Relationship to Early Reading," *Journal of Educational Psychology* 86, no. 2 (1994): 221-34; Marilyn Adams, *Beginning to Read: Thinking and Learning about Print* (Cambridge, MA: MIT Press, 1990), 80.

Table 4
Allocation of $500,000 Levy Funds,
Kennewick School District, 1996-97

Category	Dollars Allocated	Percentage
Individual Building Funds	190,000	38%
Staff Training		
First Steps ($60,000)		
CORE ($100,000)	160,000	32%
Summer School Support	60,000	12%
Reading Foundation	35,000	7%
Misc. Training/Travel	35,000	4%
Materials	20,000	4%
TOTAL	**500,000**	**100%**

We didn't identify the schools and principals by name, because our district had never published school-by-school reports. However within days, each principal had identified his or her own school as well as those of their peers. (On the next cycle, we identified scores by school and have continued to do so ever since.) The scores provided graphic evidence of the eight-year reading spans and the number of third graders falling into first- and second-grade reading levels.

One of the most important components of the reading goal was to determine the standard on the test that students would have to meet to be "at or above grade level." After an active internal debate, we set our reading standard, which we called "grade level" at third grade/fourth month based on the NWEA grade-level equivalency conversion table.

By the end of February 1996, the emotional outbursts were changing to productive effort. Most elementary principals reallocated discretionary funds and personnel to reading. About half of the schools began the gradual process of expecting/requiring parents to read twenty minutes a day with their children.

Also that month, the board earmarked $500,000 from an upcoming local levy election for the reading goal. This sum averaged about $125 per K-3 child. The question, "You mean 90% are not reading at grade level?" surfaced at almost every community forum, including the newspaper editorial board. As it happened, earmarking the levy was only symbolic evidence that the board was willing to "put its money where its mouth is" since, under Washington law, no money from that levy was available until spring of 1997. Because part of the funds was used to offset cuts by the state legislature, only $150,000 (about $37.50 per child) actually became available. The board thereafter passed a resolution dedicating those funds to reading, thus making them similar to the nondiscretionary funds earmarked for union contracts.

We were fortunate on the next step as well. When our district adopted a reading goal, elementary teachers began informally asking board members and their school leaders for help in enlisting community and parental support. What happens outside the school hours dramatically impacts classroom learning.

In February 1996, key community leaders officially organized the Reading Foundation, an area-wide nonprofit corporation with a double mission: (1) supporting schools so that all students will read at or above grade level, and (2) supporting parents in reading with their children twenty minutes a day from birth.

In May 1996, Mario Moreno, U.S. Assistant Secretary of Education, visited the Tri-Cities area to kick off the foundation's efforts to encourage family reading. The foundation distributed 15,000 copies of the U.S. Department of Education's *READ*WRITE*NOW!* activity booklets which give concise and useful suggestions to parents about how to raise a reader. Local radio stations, TV, cable, and newspapers enthusiastically promoted reading themes during the summer, providing the equivalent of $120,000 in in-kind contributions. (See Chapter 9.) Chapter 8 details why parents are critical partners in this goal. Chapter 14 provides the nuts and bolts of how the foundation was legally organized, funded, and operated.

Meanwhile, from January to June 1996, the thirteen elementary buildings in our district worked seriously on reading in K-3. Not all of the schools had a program with which they were happy. Not all of our teachers were believers. Not all of the parents were sup-

Linda McCalmant, a fourth-grade teacher at Amistad Elementary, saw three good things happening. First, "the whole school mobilized to support the reading goal" with the intermediate level teachers giving up their own paraprofessional and reading specialist resource as a deliberate investment in the quality of education for the first three grades. It created team thinking and team spirit. Second, after sifting through a lot of curriculum choices, her school chose a base program used throughout the building that "promoted continuity" but left the teachers free to go beyond it. And third, the district's commitment to pay for teacher training "helps us know we are valued members of this program."

Table 5
Percentage[1] of Kennewick Third Graders
Meeting the District Reading Standard[2] on
Functional Level Reading Tests, Spring 1996-98

School	Spring 1996	Spring 1997	Spring 1998	F & R[3]	F & R at Standard[4] Spring, 1998
Amistad	66%	65%	55%	72%	43%
Canyon View	71%	66%	78%	32%	68%
Cascade	78%	79%	72%	16%	60%
Eastgate	53%	55%	52%	67%	43%
Edison	66%	68%	71%	38%	73%
Hawthorne	84%	69%	62%	42%	50%
Lincoln	79%	75%	73%	37%	57%
Ridge View	80%	69%	78%	19%	40%
Southgate	92%	80%	81%	15%	75%
Sunset View	82%	86%	92%	4%	75%
Vista	83%	73%	90%	39%	90%
Washington	72%	72%	68%	43%	67%
Westgate	58%	55%	47%	68%	45%
District	**74%**	**70%**	**71%**	**39%**	**56%**

[1] Percentages are figured based on all third-grade students enrolled.
[2] Kennewick's reading standard for spring of third grade is an NWEA RIT score of 194. RIT figures are the basic statistic used by the Northwest Evaluation Association's functional level test to measure student growth.
[3] Percentage of children enrolled in the free or reduced (F&R) school lunch program.
[4] Percentage of children reading at or above grade level who are enrolled in the F&R lunch program.

portive. There was no additional funding. There was not even a full year in which to work. Yet in six months, the percentage of third-graders district-wide who were reading at grade level as the school year ended was up from 59% to 74%. The celebration was immense! (See Table 5 for the not pretty reality of school-by-school scores over three years.)

In 1997 the district became one of twenty-three school districts nationwide to receive a Magna Award for Outstanding Programs in School Governance for the reading goal, a national award presented by the *American School Board Journal* and Sodexho Marriott Services. As Dan Mildon, then president of our school board, commented modestly, "We don't need a national award to tell us we're going in the right direction, but it's still nice."

Several schools did far better than the economic indicators would have predicted. Hawthorne Elementary, for example, is a lower socioeconomic school where over 92% of the students who had been at Hawthorne two or more years scored at or above grade level.

Being the Flag-Bearer of Hope

Terry Barber, Principal, Amistad Elementary,
National Distinguished Principal of the Year, 1995

Perhaps you work in a school similar to mine: a high turnover rate, high student participation in the free and reduced-cost lunch program, and a growing second-language population. These indicators signify challenges that usually stretch and pull staff members.

Then, on top of this, what if your school board announced a reading goal that 90% of third graders are to be at grade level within three years?

Would you be worried, angry, frustrated?

I was.

Is the challenge reasonable and attainable?

I believe it will be difficult. I believe we will make it.

Has it been easy so far?

No.

Have we gotten there?

No.

Have we made progress toward achieving this goal?

Yes!

Attempting to reach such a goal requires us to ask important questions, to be informed, and to act on that information. In schools that are "impacted," it is especially important for the principal to be the flag-bearer of hope.

Former dissident Vaclev Havel, now president of the Czech Republic, wrote stirringly: "Hope [is] an ability to work for something to succeed. Hope is definitely not the same thing as optimism. It's not the conviction that something will turn out well, but the certainty that something makes sense, regardless of how it turns out. It is this hope, above all, that gives us strength to live and continually try new things, even in conditions that seem . . . hopeless."

While our school has not yet achieved the goal, I believe it is something that will happen. With a continued focus, unwavering effort, and a sense of hope, we can give the children who have the greatest need in our society the greatest gift—a gift that will last a lifetime: the ability to read.

There is no "riding off into the sunset" in public education. In September 1996, school began again. We tested the incoming third graders. This class scored substantially below the previous third-grade class—our first indication that the second- and first-grade teachers had not engaged reading skills with the same effectiveness as our third-grade teachers. The board continued holding its monthly workshops with elementary schools. By now, most schools had enlisted parents, urging them to do "parent homework" of reading twenty minutes a day with their children. A fraction of parents were still communicating the message, "We raise 'em. You teach 'em." These parents increasingly heard the message at parent-teacher conferences: "It is the expectation of our school board, and our community, and the principal at this school, and it is the expectation in this class that parents will read twenty minutes a day to their child." Overwhelmingly, parents were eager and supportive.

> "The Cheshire cat told Alice in Wonderland, 'It doesn't matter which way you go if you don't care about your destination.' As teachers, we do care, and the way we work together to get to a specific destination is important. As professionals, we too often do our part of educating the student in isolation. The district goal has made us realize that we have to have the whole map in mind to get our little travelers to their destination: 90% reading at grade level by the end of third grade. That goal should help us focus on working better as a team within buildings as well as across the district."
>
> —Jan Slagle, Title 1 reading teacher at Amistad Elementary, Kennewick

Schools, accountable for choosing what worked for their students, generally swung toward highly structured programs for their most impacted children,[3] although virtually every school and classroom used combinations of many elements from many programs. Very gutsy innovations flourished. When Paul Rosier, superintendent of schools, visited Amistad Elementary, he scheduled time to read to the kindergarten students. In one school, every adult—including para-professionals, principals, PE teachers, and music teachers—taught reading in small class units for two hours each morning. Another school organized a class for the parents of children who were struggling. Most schools started two-hour summer programs ($4,600 of levy dollars per school) for first- and second-grade children with reading problems.

---

[3] Barbara A. Foorman, Jack M. Fletcher, David J. Francis, Christopher Schatschneider, "The Role of Instruction in Learning to Read: Preventing Failure in At-Risk Children," *Journal of Educational Psychology* 90, no. 1 (1998): 37-55, report advantages for explicit over embedded phonic instruction for at-risk children.

First Father

Dr. Donald Fekete, retired superintendent of Finley School District, tells this story. When he keynoted the "Partnership for Learning" breakfast attended by community members from local school districts, he stressed the need for parents to spend twenty minutes a day reading aloud with children and helping their children with homework in the evenings.

After the presentation, a disgruntled listener came up and asked in a hostile tone, "What are we paying teachers for? I shouldn't be expected to help my child at home. Are you going to pay me?"

Don replied, "No, I thought it would be something you would want to do as a parent."

"No way," snapped the man. "That's what I send 'em to school for. I send them to school to learn."

Don explained: "Students who do well in kindergarten and first grade have parents who read to them. They see their parents reading at home—showing them that reading and learning are lifelong behaviors. You don't wait until you get to school to start reading to them, and you don't stop when the school bell rings at the end of the day."

The man was listening. Don concluded, "We don't advocate that parents sit down and formally instruct their preschoolers in reading. The idea is just to read to them. As a by-product, the children learn a love of reading. They develop a desire to learn to read themselves. And then, at some future wonderful moment, they will read to you instead of you reading to them."

Second Father

The Kennewick School Board heard about another victory just a few months later from a young divorced father, nervous at telling his story but speaking with riveting earnestness. He had frequent visitations with his preschool son, Jason, but he never really knew quite what to do. So Jason spent time "at" Dad's, but not time "with" Dad. Dad was frustrated, but at a loss to know what to do.

Jason was in an Early Childhood Educational Assistance Program, a project run by the Kennewick School District. The mother, as custodial parent, received the home visits, but the father started dropping in at the classroom. He loved seeing Jason interact with the other children, observed the different styles of behavior management the teachers used, and recognized quickly how much the children enjoyed being read to.

But what really made the difference was when Jason started bringing his books from the family educator on visits to his father. He insisted on being read to, and he insisted on hearing the same books over and over. The father didn't really like being "forced" to read to his son, but he found he was enjoying having Jason sit on his lap during their reading time. He realized he was getting a lot from the experience, and that he and Jason were growing closer. Sharing stories was cementing their father-son relationship. They began visiting the public library, shopping for books together, and building "Jason's library" at the father's house. Reading together had helped an unsure father discover that there's a lot to do "with" a preschooler.

The Reading Foundation, instead of putting on a few large media events, opted for numerous, smaller, energetic events with the same message, "Read with your child—the most important 20 minutes of your day."

In May 1997, we retested our graduating third-grade class—the second to go through this process. The over-all average was 70%. The good news was that this was a 16% increase from September to May. The bad news was that, overall, this was a 4% drop from the last year— 160 children away from the 90% grade level reading goal.

In August 1997, eight elementary schools participated jointly in a K-5 teacher training program called CORE, Consortium on Reading Excellence, Inc., and five schools participated in First Steps training, an Australian approach to initial reading.

Patricia Lorenz, a librarian at Ridge View Elementary invited district officers to its Finale. Each grade had its own bright color from which to fashion a chain: one link for every hour of reading, accumulated in twenty-minute increments. These students, as of April 1998, had constructed a colorful chain of 32,497 loops, stored for the most part by being tacked to the library ceiling. At its end-of-the-year party, the students were going to "circle the outside of the building with the chain," then continue the festivities with magic tricks, popsicles, and a school talent show. The students don't know it, but those vivid paper chains are linking them to a brighter future.

The training was a significant step toward team building. By this time, the instructional approach in almost every school started with phonemic awareness, progressed to imbedded or explicit phonics, and then moved from the mechanics of letters and sounds to their meaning, whether they were using First Steps or using CORE.

In September 1997, we tested our third class of third graders, conducted board workshops and teacher training, adapted curriculum approaches to student needs, and encouraged parent reading—relentlessly. In May 1998, 71% of the district's third graders scored at or above grade level with Vista Elementary at 90% and Sunset Elementary at 92%.

Each September and each May, we will continue to test. More of our schools will see 90% of our students reading at grade level. Child by child, school by school, literacy will become a skill, not a dream.

CHAPTER EIGHT

GETTING PARENTS INVOLVED

"We are a society that gives money and things to our children when what they need is our time."

—Meg Weiss, Richland School Board

Something wonderful is happening behind the milky stare of the newborn, the unblinking inspection of the toddler, and the mirthful gaze and giggles of the three-year-old. The brains of these little human beings are never more amazing than during the first three years of life when they absorb and process information in ways we are only now beginning to understand. Even before children can utter their first syllables, pathways in their brains are building connections over which language will travel, perhaps beginning with the ability to recognize vowels by the age of six months. This step may be the most basic building block of literacy.[1] (See "Build a Better Brain" at the end of this chapter.) And it occurs years before kindergarten starts.

"Parents need to take equal responsibility with schools and read to their kids."

—Governor Gary Locke, Washington State, *Tri-City Herald*, Sept. 5, 1997

Talking and reading aloud to a newborn through the preschool years develops those crucial brain structures, builds vocabulary, adds knowledge, and lengthens attention span, while teaching how to use and appreciate

---

[1] See J. Madeleine Nash, "Fertile Minds," *Time Magazine*, Feb. 3, 1997, 50-56.

How to Give Your Child
a Quarter Million Dollar Gift

High school Graduation and Lifetime Earnings[1]

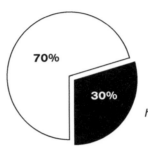

Individual lifetime
earnings of
high school graduates
$964,000

70%

30%

Individual lifetime
earnings of
high school drop-outs
$630,000

The earning difference is $334,000
*At third grade, we can predict 75% of those who will graduate and
70% of those who will drop out of high school primarily from their high and
low reading and language skills.*[2]

Third Grade Reading Levels[3]

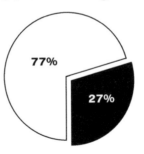

Students reading
at second to
eighth grade level
at the beginning of
third grade

77%

27%

Students reading
at kindergarten or
first grade level at
the beginning of
third grade

*A mom or dad, sister or brother, who reads twenty minutes a day with
a child from birth can first increase their chance of high 3rd grade
reading skills and then of high school graduation. When that chance
increases by 2/3rds, the child's probable increased
lifetime earnings increase by $220,000.*

---

[1] *World Almanac and Book of Facts 1998*, 95, for earning levels by education levels

[2] See Dee Norman Lloyd, "Prediction of School Failure from Third Grade Data," *Educational and Psychological Measurement* 38 (1978): 1193-1200: "As the last of the primary grades, the third grade is the point at which basic reading skills have been taught (and hopefully learned), as well as the grade in which it has been estimated that 50% of future achievement patterns have been set." Predictive factors other than reading include IQ, retention, and GPA.

[3] See Chapter 3 for reading levels in grade-level equivalents.

books. Whether a child comes to school knowing that "S says ssss!" or not knowing how to open a book depends on the quantity and quality of his or her early childhood literacy encounters.

One of the best predictors of educational success is a five-year-old's reading readiness, defined as the ability to make connections among letters, sounds, and words.[2] The enjoyable act of being read to creates that readiness.

> "Early success in school depends on how children are prepared to go to school, and that happens mostly at home."
>
> —Dr. Sara Zirkle, pediatrician, Reading Foundation Board

When parents read aloud with their child just twenty minutes a day from birth, the child enters kindergarten with a minimum of 608 hours of pre-literacy experience. If her first and second grades both spend two hours a day in reading instruction, she will get just about the same number of hours.[3]

Parents may not have understood brain physiology, but they could identify the common-sense reasons without it: Play catch with your children to develop ball handling skills; swim with them to develop water safety skills; read with them to develop reading skills. "Reading, like any other skill, is mastered with practice, over a period of time, and with the help of others."[4]

The research confirming this strategy has been available for many years. In 1985 the U.S. Department of Education commissioned national experts to evaluate twenty-five years of reading research with the goal of identifying how children master reading skills. Their report, *Becoming a Nation of Readers*, concluded: "The single most important activity for building the knowledge required for eventual success in reading is reading aloud to children. This is especially so during the preschool years."[5]

When Kennewick adopted its reading goal and the board began workshops twice monthly, teachers stressed how their reading instruction was affected by what happens in the child's life outside of the school day. Professional educators recognized that they could not do it alone. The board

---

[2] According to Marilyn Jager Adams, *Beginning to Read: Thinking and Learning about Print* (Cambridge, MA: MIT Press, 1990), 55-81, the U.S. Office of Education Cooperative Research Program in First-Grade Reading Instruction (1964-67) identified the three best predictors of success in early reading as (1) prereaders' ability to recognize and name uppercase and lowercase letters, (2) prereaders' ability to discriminate phonemes auditorily, and (3) IQ.

[3] Hours read at school are calculated using a 2 hour day x 180 days a year times 2 years = 720 hrs.

[4] Deborah Davis and Jan Patricia Lewis, *Tips for Parents about Reading* (Portland, OR: Northwest Regional Educational Laboratory's Comprehensive Center, Region X, 1997), 3.

[5] Richard C. Anderson, Elfrieda H. Hiebert, Judith A. Scott, and Ian A. G. Wilkinson, *Becoming a Nation of Readers: The Report of the Commission on Reading* (Champaign-Urbana, IL: Center for the Study of Reading, 1985), 23; emphasis ours. The first sentence quoted in this statement is Carol Chomsky, "Stages in Language Development and Reading Exposure," *Harvard Educational Review* 42 (1972): 1-33.

Carol Rasco, left, with Nancy Kerr at America Reads Challenge briefing, the White House, July 28, 1997.

READ*WRITE*NOW!

*READ*WRITE*NOW!* materials are prepared as a joint project by the U.S. Department of Education, the American Library Association, Pizza Hut, Scholastic Inc., and Reading Is Fundamental. This outstanding resource provides forty pages of practical information and ideas to use with children, grouped for prereaders, beginning readers (preschool through second grade), and young readers (grades 3-6). Another publication, *READY*SET*READ*, is designed specifically for preschoolers. It includes a calendar suggesting dozens of ideas for engaging children in language activities, and a growth chart containing important developmental information.

Reading Foundation volunteers distribute these booklets in English and Spanish when talking to parents at community events and promoting the importance of summer reading.

For more information, contact:
Carol H. Rasco, Director
The America Reads Challenge
400 Maryland Ave., SW. Room 7 West 201
Washington, DC 20202
phone: (202) 401-8888; fax: (202) 401-0596
e-mail: America_Reads_Challenge@ed.gov
Website: www.ed.gov/inits/americareads

promised teachers that they would get community support for the reading goal. From that promise, the Reading Foundation was formed.

The Reading Foundation adopted as its slogan: "The most important 20 minutes of your day . . . read with your child." The magic of this process is the simplicity of action. Any adult can do it, in just about any place, with little or no expense. It doesn't matter what language is spoken or even if the parent knows how to read. Nonreading parents can make up stories to go with the illustrations. The essential element is scheduled time with books and a positive attitude!

> "The Reading Foundation enables a district to receive services to involve the number one educator of children: the parent. Through joint efforts, parents, the schools, and the community collectively and in partnership provide the number one indicator of success to children: reading ability."
> —Dale Clark, Superintendent, Washtucna and Kahlotus School District

Parents know they are successful when they can't keep story time to just twenty minutes, and when their children beg for "just one more, please!" It's this pleasure of sharing books together that creates lifetime readers. As long as the interaction is happy, there is no way to do it wrong, although some studies show that there may be ways to do it better.[6]

To assist parents who want to expand and enrich their reading fun, our Reading Foundation distributes the U.S. Department of Education's READ*WRITE*NOW! materials. These booklets are packed with easy, enjoyable, and effective activities that fit naturally into a family's reading routine. The Reading Foundation also provides parent education materials, books to needy families, and lists of age-appropriate books kids enjoy. It coordinates and facilitates many low-cost, high-involvement activities to encourage reading to children within the community.

Beyond the benefits of becoming a future reader, reading together is a wonderful two-way opportunity for parent-child relationship building and emotional bonding. Increased love and understanding are the precious by-products of daily reading. In our haste-bedeviled, much-interrupted lives, twenty minutes is a significant commitment for parents. By example, parents communicate their own values and priorities to their children. Daily time with books tells a child that "you are very important to me" and "reading is a very important thing to do."

---

[6] Reading books whose vocabulary is slightly more advanced than the child's, and pausing to ask the child open-ended questions—"so what do you think will happen next?" or "Why did Pooh Bear do that?" create additional gains in comprehension and vocabulary.

When Parents Don't Help

Marlys Mayer, a teacher at Edison Elementary, expected challenges when she learned that only nine of her twenty-six fourth-graders were reading on grade level. What she didn't expect was a staggering lack of parental support. Sadly, she reported, "For three months I sent home a weekly reading calendar, asking parents to read to or with their children for just twenty minutes a day. I collected these calendars each Friday and checked them off. The most I ever got back was twelve. Last week, I only got back four. I sent reminder letters home and even wrote notes on the report card when the reading wasn't being done, but it did no good whatsoever." She was worried. "We need a lot more help to get these students caught up."

Another dedicated fourth/fifth grade teacher, Heidi Usher at Southgate Elementary, spelled out the "direct correlation" she saw between the parent's effort and the child's success. Sandwiched between the "really supportive parents" were those who complained about nightly reading or signing assignment sheets to verify reading homework. She also worried about older students who "start faking it as they approach middle school because a lot of adults assume their child has learned to read and they no longer read aloud."

Even after children are reading well, it is important to continue reading aloud together. School class time is limited and practice time at home is essential. According to a 1996 study, Reading Literacy in the United States, "fourth-grade average reading scores were 46 points below the national average where principals judged parental involvement to be low, but 28 points above the national average where parental involvement was high—a difference of 74 points. Even when other factors such as parents' education were taken into account, the phenomenon remained."[7] Again and again, research weighs in on one side: parent involvement makes a significant difference.

How and Why to Read Aloud

The Read Aloud Handbook by Jim Trelease (4th ed., New York: Penguin Books, 1995) documents the importance of reading and presents a smorgasbord of read-aloud books. For information about Jim Trelease's publications and cassettes contact Reading Tree Productions, 51 Arvesta Street, Springfield, MA 01118; Phone 413-782-5839, Fax 413-782-0862, http://www.trelease-on-reading.com

[7] *Reading Literacy in the United States* (Washington, DC: U.S. Department of Education, Office of Educational Research and Improvement, 1996), (NCES-96-25R), as qtd. in "President Clinton's America's Reading Challenge," flier, U.S. Department of Education, Region X, Office of Public Affairs, Jan. 15, 1997, p. 1.

For children born in this generation the ability to read well is imperative for success in school and in life. Educators who are well trained and current on reading strategies retain the responsibility of teaching children how to read. But everyone, especially parents, can assure that a child is ready to read by enjoying books together every day. The Reading Foundation unites the schools and community in providing parents the information and support they need to raise a reader.

A family who recently immigrated from Russia enjoys books together at home in Kennewick.

Photo by Rochelle Bland

There is no country in the history of the world which has successfully educated its children without involving its homes. Making parents a child's first and best teacher must become a reality.

Build a Better Brain

Before Birth

The brain creates itself. The physical capability of reading is hard-wired into the brain. Three weeks after conception, the unborn baby's brain begins creating itself by producing 15 million nerve cells (neurons) an hour. They organize themselves into two cerebral hemispheres and a "neural tube" that will become the spinal column. Bearing specific instructions, they migrate to distant parts of the developing brain and there perform specialized functions that will allow later developments to materialize. By the time the embryo is ten weeks old, these neurons are sending pulsating waves of electrical activity which physically create pathways in the mind. The brain shapes itself.

As the brain develops, it bulges in the neural tube to become the forebrain, midbrain, and hindbrain. The forebrain and midbrain govern memory, learning, interpretation, reason, IQ, and personality. The hindbrain governs unconscious functioning like reflexes, vision, hearing, posture, and breathing.

By Birth

The baby's brain contains 100 billion neurons and ten times that many glial ("glue") cells that protect and nourish them. They vary in size, depending on specialization. As few as 8 of the large ones and as many as 160 of the small ones can fit on the period at the end of this sentence. Each neuron will eventually be "wired" to thousands of other neurons.

Axons and dendrites create this "wiring." Axons are spindly signal-senders that reach out toward shorter, bushy dendrites. Sending the electrical impulse across the gap to make the connections between the cells creates a communication structure with a built-in gap called a synapse. The brain makes trillions more of these connections than it can use. The axons can be as short as one-eighth inch and as long as two inches.

As the neurons create synapses, they begin "firing" (sending electrical impulses), forming and layering the networks in the brain. The brain first makes networks required for survival (heartbeat, breathing, etc.), which are controlled by the hindbrain and midbrain.

Connecting the Brain

When the baby is about six months old, the number of connections between the neurons in parts of his or her brain explodes at a phenomenal rate, from approximately 2,500 per neurons to as many as 15,000 per neuron. A two-year-old's brain contains twice as many synapses and consumes twice as much energy as an adult brain.

Genetics seems to determine the original programming for the number of connections, but the child's sensory experience from that

Build a Better Brain

point on controls not only their number but also their size and strength. A caring, stimulating environment increases a brain's size (in a laboratory animal, a neglected brain is 20-30% smaller than normal), weight, number of neural connections, and ultimately its complexity and raw intelligence.

The Brain Starts School

From birth to age nine are irreplaceable years for brain development. Vision, hearing, touch, large muscle control, and small muscle skill all develop at the same time as the baby learns to pay attention to the sights and sounds around him or her, make decisions, process information, and form those patterns of connected images, symbols, memories, needs, desires, ideas, and emotions that make him or her into a human being, capable of interacting with others who have the same complex connections.

With each physical stimulation comes an emotional one. The brain stores both. These connections between experience and emotion, researchers feel, let children exercise judgement, connect with the values of their family, understand their communities, and contribute to society.

If a child has excellent neurological equipment, he or she can probably master appropriate developmental tasks even if the nurturing he or she receives is mediocre. But for those with more marginal abilities, some intellectual and emotional aspects that make us fully human may never develop without excellent caregiving.

In this context, spending twenty minutes a day consistently in happy reading, explaining, joking, and questioning physically alters the way a child's brain is wired. And these effects are permanent. There are "learning windows" for some skills. Children effortlessly absorb the syntactical rules of their mother tongue (or more than one) by age five or six; after that point, rules for forming sentences have to memorized and remembered.

And those preschool years are crucial. At about age ten, the brain begins a ruthless process of eliminating the less used synapses. (This physiological fact may explain why remediation, which usually starts in the fourth grade, is such hard work and why it is so seldom completely successful.) By about age eighteen, the brain's internal pathways are carved out. For better or worse, the child's unique physiology and personality are set.

Build a better brain! Read to your child!

Sources: J. Madeleine Nash, "Fertile Minds," *Time Magazine*, Feb. 3, 1997, 50-56; Stanley I. Greenspan, M.D., with Beryl L. Benderly, *The Growth of the Mind* (Reading, Mass.: Addison-Wesley, 1997).

CHAPTER NINE

INVITING COMMUNITY PARTICIPATION

"I took off September 6 from Washington, D.C., and I've seen a lot of programs, but I haven't seen a program that is really as cutting edge as this program is. I think it is further along than most because the community has genuinely gotten behind this issue. . . . Out here without any kind of resources to speak of, you all have come together and have created a program that is successful. And it's one that can be replicated in other parts of the country. You should be very proud of that."

—G. Mario Moreno, U.S. Assistant Secretary of Education
Kennewick-Pasco Rotary Meeting, September 17, 1997

Reading is the perfect community undertaking. No one is against children or reading! Absolutely no one! It is completely uncontroversial. Everyone understands the value of reading. The majority of folks in our communities are not raising young families and are not classroom teachers, yet they care deeply about children and understand the value of literacy. They welcome the opportunity to be involved.

A reading goal can unite the entire community in helping young readers, but it takes a little organization. The Reading Foundation is a "little organization" that mobilizes community awareness and support for literacy. Families and schools retain responsibility for assuring that children learn to read well, but everyone can play an essential role in helping them reach the reading goal.

The reasons for engaging parents have been discussed in Chapter 8. The legal process of organizing a nonprofit entity is discussed in Chapter 14. In this chapter, like the Kennewick School District story in Chapter 7, we are sharing the Reading Foundation story in hopes that it will provide a path for you.

Mario Moreno gives Hispanic parents in the Mid-Columbia area the same message his mother gave him: "Si, se puede! (Yes, you can.)"

In December 1995, when Kennewick adopted its Reading White Paper outlining the need to change its internal expectations, the final section dealt with external expectations: the involvement of parents and community. The White Paper recognized a clear need to increase the commitment and resources of parents to read with their children every day.

There were several initial obstacles to Kennewick's initiative to address this need.

1. Public schools are reluctant to tell parents what to do.

2. Kennewick is in a media market which includes at least nine other school districts. Any message going to Kennewick's parents would go to the parents in adjacent districts. How would those schools feel about it?

3. Portions of our populations move between the districts. Kennewick's third grader may have been Richland's preschooler and Burbank's first grader. The message needed broader coverage than just Kennewick.

4. The ability to sustain the message depended upon the buy-in of the neighboring school districts.

5. There is a competitiveness between our school districts, growing in part out of our high school sports. This attitude needed to be minimized.

The value of including other school districts was obvious. In February 1996, a separate entity—the Reading Foundation—was formed. Five districts were charter members, and five more joined in the following months. The initial five-member executive board used the membership dues to hire an interim executive director, Deb Bowen. She produced a brochure clarifying our mission, solidified the organizational structure, and identified community and national resources to support our mission. She also planned the event that publicly launched the Reading Foundation.

Financing the Reading Foundation

The Reading Foundation is a grassroots, nonprofit organization that provides services to the parents of the ten participating school districts in its region and media market. It was formed by community members, superintendents, and school board members with the goal of involving the community in supporting the local district's reading goals—specifically by educating parents about the importance of daily reading with their children. Member school districts pay one dollar per student as dues to help fund the Reading Foundation's dual mission "to assure that every child is read to twenty minutes a day and that every child reads at grade level upon completion of third grade." For each dollar of district dues, the Reading Foundation returns:

$1 in cash donations from business
$3 in media time from newspapers, TV, and radio stations
$6 in time and materials from clubs and organizations
23 volunteer hours in reading time of parents to children

In addition, there is another $2-4 of benefit per dollar of dues which comes from the "shifting" of resources. Book drives which move 20,000 young readers' books from homes with grown children into the homes of younger children shift an estimated $100,000 worth of resources. Locating high-quality media messages developed by national organizations like the American Library Association for use by local stations and the local distribution of quality training materials, such as the READ*WRITE*NOW booklets developed by the U.S. Department of Education, are other examples of shifting resources.

The official kick-off took place on May 7, 1996. Mario Moreno, U.S. Assistant Secretary of Education, spent the day in the Tri-Cities, meeting with business leaders, media representatives, and educators promoting the importance of literacy. He told the story of his own childhood, in which his mother required that he and his brother read to her and explain their homework every single night. She encouraged them, *"Si, se puede!* (Yes, you can!),"* teaching them that with determination and effort they could be successful.

That summer, the foundation promoted summer reading activities and organized its board of directors. At the end of the summer, Phelps Shepard, director of the Mid-Columbia Library system, wrote, "Summer reading participation was up by 9% in all ten of our branches and up by 21% in Kennewick. While there were a number of factors contributing to this increase, we often heard that the publicity and emphasis of the Reading Foundation made people realize just how vitally important it is to develop reading skills. We could not agree more with your basic message."

> *"We joined the Reading Foundation out of foresight. The state's K-4 Reading Accountability legislation requires every school board to set a three-year district-wide goal to increase the percentage of students who meet or exceed the fourth-grade reading standard. We knew we needed to get parents and the community involved."*
>
> —Dr. Ray Tolcacher, Superintendent
> Prosser School District

In September 1996, the Reading Foundation's full board, comprising fifteen members, met for the first time. A superintendent was invited to serve on the board as liaison with the other superintendents. At this first meeting, board members elected officers and authorized hiring a permanent part-time executive director. Since then, with Nancy Kerr as its president, the foundation has operated under four guiding principles:

> *"The Reading Foundation fills a unique niche in the Tri-Cities. While our schools focus on K-12, the Reading Foundation focuses on birth through kindergarten. Additionally it continually reinforces the importance of parents reading to their children at all ages."*
>
> —Dr. Richard Semler, Superintendent,
> Richland School District

1.   **Support families.** It is parents who have the greatest love and concern for their children and who are most likely to read to their children from birth through third grade. Our message will be directed primarily to them. We pursue leveraged ways to provide parents with the information and resources they need to raise a reader. Activities that reach the most parents with the fewest dollars will have priority.

2.   **Involve broadly.** We will encourage everyone—parents, schools, community members, and community groups—to recognize their important role in helping young readers. We will facilitate partnerships within

the community that support families, preschools, and our member school districts. Rather than a few elegant and gala events put on by foundation staff, we will find multiple pathways involving networks of people.

3. **Operate lean.** We are not a fund-raising organization. We will staff and maintain overhead at the level of the dues from our member school districts. Rather than spending half of our time fund raising, we will spend almost all of our time facilitating the donations and efforts of others in hundreds of projects. We will not duplicate, judge, or compete with services already being provided by schools, such as curriculum materials, reading programs, etc.

4. **Stay focused.** We will support only events that specifically address our narrow mission—that of parents, family members, and others reading to children every day and of schools teaching to high standards. We will check our effectiveness by asking ourselves, "Where today can parents hear the message to read with their children?" We will measure our success by how many parents read to their children and by how many third graders read at grade level.

Illinois Districts Start Reading Foundation

As superintendents, we are united in strongly endorsing the Zion-Benton Community Reading Foundation. We know that one's ability to read is the foundation for success as an adult. Yes, teaching children to read is a critical responsibility of our teachers. However, we also know that if we as a community of adults model a passion for reading, our children will follow.

So ... we encourage everyone–parents and family members, church congregations, senior citizens, government officials, educators, preschool teachers, coaches–to get involved. Our children do what they see. Let's show them how much all of us as adults value reading and academic excellence.

Larry Fleming, Superintendent
Beach Park District 3

Jim Taylor, Superintendent
Zion District 6

Bud Marks, Superintendent
Winthrop Harbor District 1

Gary Fields, Superintendent
Zion-Benton Township High School

Through public speaking, media interviews, newsletters, and other opportunities that come their way, foundation officers and board members share their important message. Civic groups, service clubs, religious institutions, nonprofit agencies, professional organizations, and businesses have responded with ideas and offers that far exceed our own vision. They eagerly sponsor projects suited to the distinctive resources and interests of their membership and employees. This ownership, coupled with genuine concern for children and literacy, is synergistic.

Have you read with a child today?

Outlined at the end of this chapter is a chronology of the foundation's activities from its beginning until this book went to press. We hope it suggests how a Reading Foundation in your own community can replicate these results. It tells the story of how two part-time people—the president and executive director[1]—can generate a powerful literacy message with the support of many wonderful community partners and competent media reporters. Just a few projects each month can create the needed impact.

Boosting the quality and quantity of family reading time requires forging hundreds of links between our ideas, our institutions, and our practices. Reading Foundation projects forge those links. Employers encourage employees to read with their children. Medical professionals promote reading as part of a healthy lifestyle. New mothers and fathers go home with "Read to Me" bibs embroidered by hands now two generations old. Teenagers tackle service projects that assist young readers. The value of literacy is preached from the pulpit and proclaimed over loudspeakers at baseball games. City officials approve road signs reminding citizens to read with a child every day. Service clubs provide books that beginning readers cherish.

Despite the dynamic impact of the Reading Foundation during its first two and a half years, there are still unmet needs and opportunities, many almost invisible in the community for years. These include:

Visit the Reading Foundation's website at *www.ReadingFoundation.org for information about community service ideas, reading aloud with your child, and legislation.*

First, this vibrant message about literacy is primarily reaching the converted or almost-converted—those who read newspapers and watch En-

---

[1] A teacher in the Kennewick School District, Nancy Kerr was given a half-day released time to develop community participation in the 90% reading goal. Erin Tomlinson, the executive director, works three-quarters time.

glish TV news. The months ahead will bring programs for Hispanic, Russian, Bosnian, and Asian immigrants. Board members are carefully preparing so that they will understand how to work respectfully with these cultures, in addition to providing appropriate books and translated materials.

Second, a whole generation of future parents is "right under our noses" in school every day. We want to provide students with information and experiences so they will leave high school knowing why and how to raise the next generation of readers.

Third, the foundation wants to encourage other regions to meet the same critical need, to tap the same enormous reservoir of concern and good will. Its "Reading Foundation in a Box" is a way of giving other communities a jump start on their own foundations. (See Chapter 14.)

Says Erin Tomlinson, the foundation's executive director, "The Reading Foundation's message can be incorporated into every activity in town. In this era of educational reform, we will only be able to make the progress needed if we all work together. We can solve the problem of literacy when all of us—families, schools, and communities—feel the power of our unique roles."

The Reading Foundation creates the framework to establish a community of readers. Parents and communities are the foundation of this reading effort.

A Three-Year Calendar of Reading Foundation Activities

1996

MARCH

- The Reading Foundation (RF) five-member steering committee stabilizes its message and approach, completes brochure, logo, and by-laws.

MAY

- U.S. Assistant Secretary of Education Mario Moreno kicks off the RF with an all-day visit, which includes a press conference, two luncheons with key business leaders, taping four public service announcements (PSAs) and visiting schools. Receives widespread media coverage and front page of *Tri-City Herald*.

- A *Tri-City Herald* editorial supports the Reading Foundation's message.

"Businesses need an educated workforce. Low reading expectations cheat kids and, ultimately, society."

—Sandra Matheson, CEO, Hanford Environmental Health Foundation and Vice President of the Reading Foundation

---

- A marketing class at the Washington State University—Tri-Cities campus creates four PSAs which begin airing on local TV stations: KEPR, KNDU, KVEW.

JUNE

- Moreno PSAs begin to run with WSU's PSAs.

- School and business marquees stress summer reading themes.

JULY

- American Library Association (ALA) PSAs with an RF tagline start airing during children's viewing times. PSAs include: "Beauty and the Beast," "Fishing with Grandpa," and "California Grapes."

- The RF executive committee invites key community leaders to serve on its board of directors.

AUGUST

- Summer reading increases 9-15% at all ten branches of the Mid-Columbia Library. The media report these statistics.

- Area businesses include the "20 minutes a day" message in employee newsletters.

- The Community Health and Safety Network provides RF with $4,500 to buy a year's supply of books for Home Health Nurses to give to 185 at-risk families at each quarterly visit.

SEPTEMBER

- Columbia Basin Community College provides a central and neutral location for RF quarterly board meetings. The first board meeting elects officers and issues a press release.

- Kennewick School District fuses vinyl signs, "Read to your child 20 minutes a day" on the sides of school buses with funding from Wal-Mart. The *Herald* runs a front-page photograph.

- The RF begins providing material for parents in Columbia Basin College's adult literacy program.

OCTOBER

- 3,000 bright yellow ALA "Kids Who Read Succeed" buttons are distributed, creating a high level of visibility throughout the community and in schools.

NOVEMBER

- The RF makes a presentation at the Washington State School Directors Association's annual conference with Kennewick School District, distributes "Kids Who Read Succeed" buttons and RF brochures.

DECEMBER

- The RF meets with Washington State Senate's Education Committee chair to explain its mission.

- Local police officers encourage daily reading on the backs of trading cards featuring their photo and information.

- The estimated value of PSAs by TCI, radio stations KONA and KORD, television stations KEPR, KNDU, and KVEW, and contributions by Northwest Public Television and the *Tri-City Herald* exceeded $94,000 for 1996.

1997

JANUARY

- Meetings advocating the third-grade reading goal and accountability, with a parent reading component, continue with Superintendent of Public Instruction Terry Bergeson, with the Chair of the Commission on Student Learning (CSL) Chuck Collins, and with the CSL executive director, House Education chair, an aide to the Lieutenant Governor, and the executive director of Washington Round Table.

- The RF is invited to join the state's "Year of the Reader" committee by the chair of the House Education Committee.

- The RF is invited to testify twice during the legislative session, once to the House Education Committee and once to the Senate Education Committee. The Tri-Cities media covers both events.

- Northwest Public Television starts monthly donation of new children's books to the RF for distribute to parents of at-risk children. PBS covers the event. Elementary teachers give the books on home visits.

- Leadership Tri-Cities Class II volunteers to build and stock a reading room for the Boys and Girls Club in Pasco.

- Goodwill Industries includes the RF presentation in its educational outreach classes. The *Herald* runs a front-page photo of the presentation.

FEBRUARY

- During an editorial board meeting with Washington's Governor Gary Locke, *Herald* publisher Ian Lamont tosses him an ALA "Kids Who Read Succeed" button across the table, commenting, "You'd better put it on. You're in reading country now."

- The Harlem Globetrotters focus on reading at assemblies in five different school districts. 4,000 kids come to evening program with their parents in Kennewick. Area-wide media coverage and front-page Herald treatment carry the message even farther.

- Richard Wright, owner of Columbia Physical Therapy, donates 1,000 basketballs to the RF for distribution to Benton City, Finley, Burbank, Pasco, and Kennewick school kids who reach reading goals with parents. Extensive media coverage.

- Washington Mutual Bank of Pasco buys and presents a new book to all 620 students at Ruth Livingston Elementary School in Pasco.

- Kennewick General Hospital includes reading as part of a healthy lifestyle in its community newsletter, *Healthbeat*. It offers the RF space on its TelMed phone lines.

"Our future depends on developing strong partnerships, such as the Reading Foundation. It takes everyone—not only parents—but grandparents, agencies, businesses, and community groups working together to establish a sound reading foundation for our children."

—Dr. Gary Henderson, Superintendent, Kiona-Benton School District

---

MARCH

- B. Dalton Bookstore hosts a "First Book" party for at-risk children invited by the RF. Media coverage.

- The RF starts a monthly literacy program at the six local Head Start sites. Children participate in literacy activities at school throughout the month, and parents are invited to a family dinner where they learn about reading aloud with their children and enjoy a story and craft with their children. Outstanding attendance.

APRIL

- The *Tri-City Herald's* "In-Touch" Storyline begins. Members of the Benton-Franklin Chapter of the International Reading Association record the stories in English and Spanish with monthly updates. KONA radio and businesses print magnets to promote the storyline. The *Herald* promotes the storyline biweekly.

Willingly Captive Audiences:
Reading at the Health and Human Services Office
and La Clinica

Almost fifty children heard stories on the first day. Some of them were the children of the many Hispanic workers attracted to the farms, orchards and vineyards of southeastern Washington.

Local school districts had asked the Reading Foundation to reinforce their efforts with migrant families, since the children often do not speak English in the home and frequently change schools before the end of the year. So the foundation initiated reading centers at the Health and Human Services Office and La Clinica (health care center) in Pasco. These locations have many at-risk children waiting for hours at a time while their parents fill out forms, wait for checks, or wait to see a doctor.

One corner of the waiting room has a bulletin board with brightly decorated and clearly captioned reading information and encouragement. But during the busiest times, usually Tuesday and Thursday afternoons from 1:00 to 3:00, bilingual readers scheduled by the Volunteer Center wheel out a cart of books and delight children and parents with stories. Then they present each child with a book donated by Northwest Public Television— with a different title every month—and parents with *READ*WRITE*NOW* kits in English or Spanish.

Welfare office manager Ann Blanchard welcomes the effort because it gives the bored and restless children something to do while their parents are occupied and because "the more successful kids are in school now, the less likely they are to be needing our services" in the future.

The result? The children have a rich literacy experience, parents see reading aloud modeled, and the family takes home a book of its own. If a love of reading is ignited by a volunteer's lively reading of Dr. Seuss, that child's world and opportunities will open up immeasurably. Education is essential to breaking the cycle of poverty.

—Mike Lee, "Welfare Office a Place for Reading," *Tri-City Herald*, Aug. 8, 1997, A-3; "Reading Program Simple, Yet Grand," Editorial, *Tri-City Herald,* Aug. 11, 1997, A-6.

- The *Herald* publishes a series of articles on reading. Governor Locke urges children to "read voraciously."

MAY

- The RF makes a presentation at the Child Care Directors Association representing over 1,000 local daycare facilities and begins providing on-going articles for the association's monthly newsletter.

- Summer Reading kick-off at Columbia Center Mall. The Volunteer Center arranges for VIPs to read to children in twenty-minute segments on a Saturday. Tri-Tech Skills Center students in its television production class video the stories and produce five 30-minute TV shows. TCI Cablevision broadcasts them 15 times a week all summer. Media coverage.

JUNE

- Boys and Girls Club reading center completed by the Leadership Tri-Cities Class II. Media coverage.

The graduation ceremonies for the Leadership Tri-Cities II class, June 1997, featured an inspiring slide presentation of the completed Boys and Girls Club reading center. Concluded Rev. Ronnie White, member of the Pasco School Board and Reading Foundation Board, "Education in the Tri-Cities—where every child learning to read is a reality, not a dream."

- McDonald's trayliners feature the winning drawing of an elementary school contest, "I like to read in the summer." Other drawings are displayed at libraries and the Columbia Center Mall.

- HAAP (Hispanic Academic Achievers Program) includes the RF and materials at its major annual celebration attended by over 1,000 parents, children, and community leaders.

"Kids who read succeed," says Ian Lamont, publisher of the Tri-City Herald and a charter member of the Reading Foundation board. "We want parents to take the time to read to their children every day. But with busy schedules, there will almost certainly be times when children want more. So we're providing the 'In-Touch' Storyline, a telephone service to allow children to have someone read them a story anytime they want."

- The RF participates in quarterly meetings with hospital personnel who teach prenatal classes, encouraging them to include a "Read to your baby 20 minutes a day" message for new parents. Training continues to present.

JULY

- The RF provides books and training to Hispanic families through Catholic Child and Family Services.

- Members of the Church of Jesus Christ of Latter-day Saints sew, decorate, and donate 500 book bags for young readers. The RF distributes them to elementary teachers in fall.

- The RF is invited to attend the White House Conference on the America Reads Challenge. The RF joins the America Reads Challenge Coalition. Media coverage.

AUGUST

- The RF starts bi-weekly (Tuesday and Thursday) Storytime at the Pasco Department of Health and Social Services Office (welfare office).

- The *Herald* editorial page praises the welfare office reading program.

- Pasco School District puts up school signs reminding citizens: "Have You Read with a Child Today?"

- The RF president and executive director meet individually with each superintendent to assure the coordination of the media messages, events, and satisfaction levels.

SEPTEMBER

- Prosser School District joins the RF and forms "Prosser Partnership for Literacy" to implement activities in their town. Media.

- Jim Trelease, author of *The Read Aloud Handbook*, accepts an invitation to appear at a community event in April 1999.

- Washington State releases the results of the statewide fourth grade reading test, considered a call for renewed efforts. District reading scores, district reading programs, and parent reading messages make the front page of the *Herald*. Media coverage continues for two weeks.

- The *Herald* editorial page discusses reading test scores and the importance of the RF message for parents.

- The *Herald* editorial page features Johns Hopkins research on reading to infants and on the RF's "20 minutes a day" reading goal.

- KONA Radio supports the RF by providing $500 of free air time for each advertiser who donates $500 to the RF: Bear-Mart Auto Sales, Boss Internet Group, Coit Carpet and Cleaning Service, Creative Travel, Granny's Buffet, Print Plus, Russ Dean Ford, Shumate Auto, Story Teller's Audio Book, Tri-City Nissan, and Windermere Real Estate participate.

- KONA announcers produce PSAs sharing their favorite childhood reading memories.

- Fluor Daniel Hanford, Inc., Waste Management Services Hanford, B&W Hanford, DE&S Hanford, Numatic Hanford, Lockheed Martin Hanford, and Bechtel Hanford donate $2,500 to the RF.

- Group Health Northwest designs and produces three brochures ("Reading to Your Baby," "Reading to Your Toddler," and "Reading to Your School-Age Child") for placement in doctors' offices in Washington, Idaho, and Oregon. It makes an unlimited number available to the RF for use.

- The Washington State Lottery donates $5,000 to RF.

- The Nike Golf Tournament includes the RF as one of five charitable causes to which the proceeds are distributed. Media coverage.

OCTOBER

- U.S. Department of Education Assistant Secretary Mario Moreno accepts the RF's invitation to visit the Tri-Cities again. He tours Pasco schools, speaks at Rotary, attends a reception at KONA Radio and produces two PSAs. Media coverage.

- "Year of the Reader" buttons are made and distributed throughout the community.

- Members of the Washington State House Education Committee tour Kennewick School District. RF helps host. Media coverage.

- A Reading Foundation booth at Family a'Fair reaches 15,000-18,000 families. Media coverage.

- Central Washington University students in the Family and Consumer Science Association create and donate puppets to go with children's storybooks.

NOVEMBER

- The RF gives training and books to the local Migrant/Bilingual Parents Council.

- The RF is invited to present at the U.S. Department of Education, Region X, and Northwest Educational Laboratory's "Taking Action to Improve Reading" Conference.

- For the grand opening of a local Barnes and Noble, the bookstore selects the RF as its local partner and includes its message in publicity.

- The Washington State Lottery gives one free ticket for each donated book brought to a Tri-City American Hockey game and gives the RF "ice time" for a half-time message. Media coverage.

- Americorps members conduct a drive for RF that collects over 6,000 "gently used" books. Media coverage.

DECEMBER

- A *Tri-City Herald* editorial supports the governor's reading program, third-grade reading goal, and RF "20 minutes a day" message.

- Barnes and Noble provides "Give a needy child a book" Christmas tree. Hundreds of new books purchased by customers are giftwrapped for the RF to distribute. Parents are encouraged to buy books as presents.

- Hanford Environmental Health Foundation employees bring books to their Christmas party to donate to the RF.

- The RF distributes books for Christmas at elementary schools in Connell and other sites.

A Family a' Fair

With the help of its community friends, the Reading Foundation shares its important message at many events. One such occasion is the annual Family a'Fair—an October weekend when 15,000-18,000 parents visit the Pasco Trade Center to get parenting information from local agencies. They bring their kids, and the Reading Foundation entertains/educates them with the reading message.

Kennewick High School students, dressed in storybook costumes, help children decorate "Read to Me" windsocks, funded by a gift from SeaFirst Bank. Every twenty minutes, a new group of kids piles on the reading bus to hear a story, providing Reading Foundation board members with an opportunity to talk to waiting parents and distribute educational materials.

The Atomic Kiwanis Club arranges for a Ben-Franklin (for Benton-Franklin Counties) Transit bus to be parked by our booth, stocked with books and VIP guest readers. Columbia Center Mall purchases the space for the Reading Foundation at the fair and provided the banner and publicity. The bus and windsocks are big attractions, and the foundation reaches many parents.

- The RF invites children to attend a Barnes and Noble "First Books" party for at-risk children. Media coverage.

- Prosser hosts a community storytime with Santa and gives away books provided by the RF. Media coverage.

- The value of PSAs by TCI, radio stations KONA and KORD, and television stations KEPR, KVET, and KNDU, and contributions by Northwest Public Television and the *Tri-City Herald* are estimated to exceed $110,000 for 1997.

Reading to Newborns

How do you persuade parents to read to newborns? Send them home from the hospital with an "I Read to My Baby" book bag. These brightly decorated plastic drawstring bags are filled with a new book (popular titles include Clifford the Red Dog series and Rosemary Wells's heart-warming *Read to Your Bunny*), the baby's first library card, a brochure from Group Health Northwest informing parents about the whys and hows of reading to their baby, and—perhaps the most adorable single item—a newborn-size handmade flannel bib with the cross-stitched slogan, "Read to Me."

Hailey Helland was Kadlec Hospital's first baby bookbag recipient. Here she models her "Read to Me" bib with parents Devin and Kristy, and siblings Ambre and Skyler in the Kadlec Birthing Center. Devin is wearing the Reading Foundation's popular button, "Read to Your Child."

United Way funded the purchase of picture books to give to the parents of babies born at Kennewick General Hospital, the Benton-Franklin Chapter of the International Reading Association donated books in English and Spanish for Our Lady of Lourdes Hospital in Pasco, and Prosser Memorial Hospital and Kadlec Hospital in Richland also acquired funding for books.

Members of local churches, high school Future Homemakers of America, the Volunteer Center's RSVP (Retired Senior Volunteer Program), and the Hospital Auxiliary ply the needles to keep the hospitals supplied with these keepsake bibs for future readers. Approximately 4,000 baby bookbags are distributed each year among the area's four hospitals.

Reading Foundation volunteers were delighted when nurses reported that some women, even in labor, have asked, "When do I get my baby's reading kit?"

1998

- The RF continues monthly participation at six Head Start evening programs, quarterly participation with the Child Care Directors Association, biweekly readings at the Department of Health and Human Services office, distribution of books provided by Northwest Public Television, and presentations to groups throughout the community.

JANUARY

- The Reading Foundation asks Washington State University—Tri-Cities campus about a survey quantifying the level of those reading twenty minutes a day. Kennewick School District begins collecting elementary school levels of parents' reading participation K-3.
- The RF joins Washington's Promise which focuses on service to young readers. General Colin Powell speaks to members in Seattle about the goals of the President's Summit for America's Future.

- The Books for Babies program starts at Kennewick General Hospital, funded by an initial $5,000 United Way grant for materials. Media coverage.
- Karate Kids hold a Kick-a-Thon at the Tri-City Court Club and raise $900 for preschool books. Media coverage.
- SeaFirst Bank donates $5,000 for books for preschoolers.
- KONA Radio continues a fundraising program for spring promotion.

FEBRUARY

- The RF and Barnes and Noble cohost a second "First Book" party for Head Start children. Media coverage.
- RF leaders attend an area-wide meeting of superintendents to report and plan activities

---

One evening I was speaking to a women's church group about the goals of the Reading Foundation. The audience consisted of women ages eighteen to eighty. During my thirty-minute presentation, I was fascinated by the women's reactions. The young mothers were serious, concentrating deeply and taking extensive notes. It was clearly important to them to understand what was happening in the schools and how they could help their children be successful. The older women were appreciative, relaxed and self-assured, frequently nodding in gentle approval. I closed by reminding everyone—mothers, grandmothers, aunts, caregivers—of the importance of reading aloud with children every day.

However, after the meeting several older women approached me, clearly agitated. "I can't believe that you actually have to go around and tell people to read to their children. For heaven's sake, when I was raising my children, every night after dinner we cleared the table and read books and played games for a couple of hours." A few other women added their wonderful memories of enjoying reading routines together with their family after the evening meal.

I commented, "Many families today don't even have dinner together, let alone story time. Our society lives differently, but family reading time is as important as ever."

—Nancy Kerr, President, the Reading Foundation

- The RF offers a class for parents through Kennewick School District's Community Schools.

MARCH

- The RF makes a presentation at S.E. Washington Title I/Migrant Bilingual Conference.
- Voters in three cities approve funding to remodel or construct five public libraries.

"The Reading Foundation is exemplary of the grassroots partnering essential to comprehensive school reform. This initiative is transformational and systemic in its approach. The vision implied harnesses the key ingredient to lasting and continual school improvement. This is a shift in culture favoring the notion that education is everyone's business and everyone's responsibility. With its simple message of "read to your children," the foundation is accomplishing something that is substantive and far reaching."

— Dr. G. Robert Van Slyke
Superintendent, Finley School District

- Girl Scout Troop 177 organizes all local troups to collects hundreds of used children's books at Round Table Pizza, local elementary schools, and Bergstrom Aircraft. Media coverage.
- Two thirty-minute interviews with RF officers air on Radiant Light, local Christian TV.
- The Center for Chiropractic Care sponsors three "gently used" bookdrives for the RF.
- Media coverage of Dr. Seuss's birthday. Local school districts promote reading through special school-site contests with the RF's help.
- The RF teams with Marriott Food Services to have school lunch personnel encourage young readers. "We want kids who are well fed and well read."

APRIL

- A Prosser grocer prints artwork of "Kids Who Read Succeed" contest winners on grocery bags. Media coverage.
- Kennewick City approves street signs that ask, "Have you read with a child today?"
- The *Herald* editorial page features "Book Day" and "20 minutes a day" reading program.
- Kennewick School District librarians volunteer to read stories for four Saturdays at Columbia Center Mall.
- The RF gives away Storyline magnets and *READ*WRITE*NOW* kits at the Tri-Cities Easter Egg Hunt.
- Kennewick High School Careers in Education students apply computer-generated graphics saying "Read to Me" to T-shirts donated by Target Stores. The shirts are given to children in Kahlotus and Washtucna.
- The RF hosts a Barnes and Noble "Babies Blossom with Books" event including a presentation by local pediatrician Dr. Sharon Ahart and a book give-away.

MAY

- Books for Babies starts at Prosser Memorial Hospital with books provided by the RF. Prosser High School Future Homemakers of America make more than 200 "Read to Me" bibs. Media coverage.
- Governor Gary Locke and Superintendent of Public Instruction Dr. Terry Bergeson celebrate children's literacy at the Columbia Center Mall at an event coordinated by the RF with Educational Service District #123 and ten districts.

After his speech, the governor sits down with a group of children and reads to them. McDonald's and Barnes and Noble provide refreshments. Entertainment includes a reading rap performed by students from Sunset Elementary in Kennewick and a calypso steel band from Richland's Tapteal Elementary School. Media coverage.

Balloons, bookmarks, and bright faces enliven the Reading Foundation's booth at the Cinco de Mayo celebration.

- The RF and Girl Scouts host a book give-away party for local Head Start children at Northwest Public TV. Media coverage.

- The *Prosser Record Bulletin* takes a strong editorial pro-reading position and reports on local businesses that support twenty minutes a day reading. For example, Brown's Tire Company keeps children's books in its customer waiting area.

- Skate West promotion allows two to skate for the price of one when customers donate a children's book.

- The RF participates in local Cinco de Mayo celebration in Pasco which attracts thousands of Hispanic families. Media coverage.

JUNE

- A read-a-thon at Columbia Center Mall kicks off the summer reading program. Local celebrities read to kids and parents. Media coverage.

- The RF distributes approximately 20,000 *READ*WRITE*NOW* booklets in ten districts to encourage summer reading.

- The RF receives a local "Literacy Award" from the Benton-Franklin Chapter of the International Reading Association. Media coverage.

- The RF receives the state "Literacy Award" from the Washington State International Reading Association. Media coverage.

- HAAP (Hispanic Academic Achievement) partnership event. RF distributes information.

- For Father's Day, the RF and Barnes and Noble host "Daddy and Me" reading time for children and their dads. The Tri-City Posse Baseball team donates baseball tickets for those who attend, so children can enjoy two of America's summertime favorites, reading and baseball. Media coverage.

- Radio and TV PSAs air featuring an "Our Time" theme for Father's Day. PSAs feature dads enjoying storytime with their children.

- The RF participates in an all-day "Children's Festival." Booth sponsored by RF board member Nolan Curtis. Media coverage.

A Focus on Quality

Bruce H. Hawkins
Superintendent, Burbank School District

I worked in a Ford garage during the early 70s. Ford was taking a pounding in car sales from Japanese and European manufacturers. Mechanics disliked the foreign cars and we charged extra for working on them. We made up unflattering nicknames for the cars and the people who bought them. In short, our response to competition was resentment and protectionism.

In 1973, I left to begin my career in education. In 1974, the oil embargo spelled a new low in car sales. In response, the Ford Motor Company began an unprecedented focus on quality and coined the phrase "Quality Job 1," a phrase it backed up with its creation of the Ford Escort. Quality has remained Ford's primary focus for the last two decades. As a result of this long-term focus, Ford has recently had several quarters where it led the world in car sales, something it hasn't done since Henry was in control.

The Reading Foundation has independently invented Ford's key to success. It has a clear and single focus. All of the local districts share its thrust. While we struggle to inform our publics about other key improvement strategies, everyone in our region knows about the Reading Foundation and "the most important 20 minutes" of the day. The media has been supportive because the approach is clear.

The Reading Foundation is powerful. Its clever marketing strategies have been important, but equally important is the passion of its people. From the interested school board member to the executive director, they have instant credibility with school and community organizations. I've never seen the public embrace a school message like "the most important 20 minutes of the day."

Public education faces many challenges. Protectionism is counterproductive. Perhaps the Reading Foundation's model shows us a better way, a clear focus on quality. And in retrospect, our schools, and our children, with the Reading Foundation have a much greater chance of reaching the reading goal than Ford ever had of regaining its No. 1 position.

- The RF coordinates with local school districts to host family reading nights to kick off summer reading.

- The RF participates in a local "Riverfest" walk-a-thon to raise money for books, an event sponsored by the *Tri-City Herald* and the Volunteer Center. Media coverage.

- Summer reading signs go up on school marquees. Horse Heaven Hills Middle School's reads: "Summer reading— summer not. RU?" Promotion by local media.

- The RF provides a box of books for Washtucna Community Pool for poolside reading.

- The RF places boxes of books in the activity centers of low-rent apartment complexes for children during the summer vacation.

- The RF distributes materials at Prosser Health Fair.

- Kadlec Hospital (Richland) starts its Books for Babies program with books provided by Kadlec Hospital Foundation. Media coverage.

JULY

- The RF and Volunteer Center partner to bring Summer Storytime to Barnes and Noble. Local teenagers read with children. Media coverage.

- A local weekly TV show showcases the RF Books for Babies program at Kadlec Hospital on its "Community Health Journal" program.

- Reader Board Campaign: Numerous local businesses display summer reading messages.

- The RF provides books and training to parents through Catholic Child and Family Services.

- The RF holds a "Beach Party" at Barnes and Noble. All kids receive a new book. Media coverage.

- RF volunteers begin biweekly story-reading to children at Pasco's La Clinica Health Care Center. Media coverage.

AUGUST

- The Washington State Lottery gives a free lotto ticket on "Reading Foundation Night" at the Tri-City Posse Baseball game to everyone who donates a child's book. In-game entertainment features "bottom of inning" child competitions for books signed by all the team players. Media coverage.

- Local high school students begin reading once a week at La Clinica Health Care Center for an entire school semester.

- SeaFirst Bank commercial highlights Reading Foundation.

- RF leaders meet individually with superintendents to assure the coordination of the media messages, media events, and satisfaction levels.

- Jared Fielding designs and launches the first version of RF webpage at www.ReadingFoundation.org

- The RF prepares book boxes for ten long rural school bus routes in Prosser.

- The Teen Parent teacher at Tri-Tech Area Skills Center shares the RF message with students, then helps them make computer-generated quilt blocks of stories they read to their baby, eventually completing a keepsake quilt.

- For "Fiesta de la Familia," hosted by Americorps, the RF provides materials in English and Spanish for hundreds of families.

- The RF distributes materials to hundreds of families at the "Fiery Food Festival" in Pasco. Pasco School District includes RF information at its booth.

- Pasco School District distributes RF information at the Benton and Franklin County Fair and Rodeo.

FALL ACTIVITIES:

- The RF provides three hours of training and activities to 1,300 student leaders at the Washington Association of Student Councils conference, focusing on how high school students can support young readers. Media coverage.
- Washington Reading Corps members begin working in local schools and providing service at RF events.

One evening I shared the Reading Foundation's message with a service organization, then answered questions while they assembled book bags for a local elementary school. One young woman, Michelle Withers, pregnant with her first child, was especially interested in learning everything about being the best possible mother.

Several months later when she gave birth to her child, he lived for only thirty minutes. Heartsick, I went to the funeral home to express my sympathy to Michelle and her husband Neil. To my amazement, she put her arms around me and said, "I'm so thankful you told me about reading to my child. I began reading to Jeremy weeks before he was born. I always knew that he heard me and knew that I loved him. I'm so grateful I read to him because it created such a loving and comforting memory for me."

Tears welled up in my eyes as she added, "You never know how much time you will have with a child. Those times we shared reading are precious memories that I'll never forget."

*—Nancy Kerr, President
the Reading Foundation*

- RF presents at the state WORD Conference (Washington Organization for Reading Development).
- The Tri-City Americans Hocky Team features RF messages at games and in programs. Players read weekly at elementary schools. Washington State Lottery sponsors book drives at three games. Media coverage.
- The Department of Energy and Fluor Daniel organize a "Thanks 4 Giving" community-wide book drive. Together, with dozens of other groups and businesses, over 70,000 "gently used" books were collected. Media coverage.
- Full-size billboards are prepared to go up on heavily traveled streets: "The most important 20 minutes of your day...READ WITH YOUR CHILD."
- RF distributes "Read with Your Child" buttons in Spanish and English for teachers to wear at fall parent conferences.
- Storybook Santa arrives at Columbia Center Mall. He encourages reading by giving books to the first 300 children. RF leaders read holiday stories to children waiting for Santa. Media coverage.
- Mona Lee Locke and Melinda French Gates (wives of Governor Gary Locke and Bill Gates) host an early childhood developmental forum organized by the Reading Foundation and other local agencies. Locke and Gates meet with community leaders and speak with parents about developmental issues. Media coverage.
- Authors send the "90% Reading Goal" book to press.

PART TWO

CREATING READING ACCOUNTABILITY

Establishing good tests, determining student achievement standards for those tests, and reporting the results are the most leveraged activities in which a legislature or school board can engage. These activities can transform a district or a state. They are unique responsibilities of governance of public education.

Part Two is the nuts and bolts of how to build reading accountability in your district. Its five chapters are process oriented and more technical, designed for board members, superintendents, and professional educators creating reading accountability policies and mechanisms in their own district. Parents, legislators, and newspaper publishers may want to just skim this section or move directly to Part Three, starting at page 141. In Part Two we explain:

- How to establish a district or state reading goal (Chapter 10)
- How to establish standards, assessments, and reporting procedures (Chapters 11-12)
- How, where, and why to reset district parameters (Chapter 13)
- How to create a reading foundation (Chapter 14)

At 300 words a minute, reading every word, the reading time for this part is 1 hour 40 minutes.

CHAPTER TEN

SETTING YOUR GOAL

> *"The task of a leader is to get his [or her] people from where they are to where they have never been."*
>
> —Henry Kissinger

Setting the district (or state) elementary reading goal is the most significant, long-term policy decision that we as boards and superintendents (or legislators) will make during our tenure. It will affect the rate of learning for 40% of the students in our schools for the rest of their lives. It will affect the range of literacy skills in every one of our classrooms. It may graduate thousands of students out of the pool of those who otherwise drop out, who are unemployable, or who fill our prisons. In setting the goal, we need to consider four questions:

1. At what percentage should the board set the goal?

2. What grade level should be the measurement point?

3. What year should the goal be achieved?

4. What process should be used in setting the goal?

> *"A goal is an end, a result, not just a task or a function to be performed. It is a place in space and time that describes the condition we want to achieve. It is a standard of achievement, a criterion of success, something tangible, measurable, and valuable that we are motivated toward. It is concrete and explicit, definitive and desirable and predetermined."*
>
> —Charles L. Hughes, *Goal Settling: Key to Individual and Organization Effectiveness* (American Management Association, 1996), 8.

Calculating the Percentage

Assume Lowell Elementary has 100 third graders in four classes of 25 students each who were tested in September. Assume also that:

5   students were absent and were not retested

7   special education students were not tested

12   were not tested because of their limited English

8   were not tested because they would do poorly

48   of the remaining 68 students, scored at or above grade level

So, if you calculate only those students who were tested, it looks as if 70.5% of Lowell's students are reading at or above grade level (48/68=70.5%). This looks pretty good. Obviously, there's room for improvement, but there's no real emergency.

Or is there? This figure masks the fact that we don't actually know how many of Lowell's students are reading at grade level because only 68% were actually tested. Each reduction introduces some degree of distortion. What if the missing 32% actually read below grade level? (Statistically, it's improbable that all of them would, but look again at the criterion for exclusion. Most of them would.) Those results would show that more than half—52% of Lowell's students—couldn't manage their own textbooks.

The cleanest, most accurate, most reproducible—and most ethical—method for reporting the number of students at or above the standard is by using 48 as the numerator, and 100 as the denominator, 48/100 for 48%:

numerator = the number of children scoring at or above the standard

denominator = all children at that grade level

Lowell can show 10% real growth in the same students by June by increasing the number of students reading above the standard by 10 (58/100 = 58%). Or Lowell can show 10% phantom growth by excluding 17 students from the denominator without improving anyone's actual reading ability. (48/(100-17) = 48/83 = 58%

When we use all students, we establish an honest baseline from which we can measure real growth. When we use all students, we eliminate the incentive to create phantom growth merely by excluding more students who would not do well on the test.

The first three questions can be summarized by selecting answers to these three questions: (1) What percentage of students should be grade-level readers? 60%? 70%? 80%? 90%? (2) By what grade should they achieve it? Second? Third? Fourth? (3) And by what year will they reach the grade level goal? In 2002? 2003? or 2004?

1.   At what percentage should the board set the goal?

A board needs to consider several intertwined issues when setting the percentage goal. It is enticing to say that "all children," meaning 100% of children, will read at grade level. It sounds wonderful. It rings with political correctness. But the truth is that an estimated 5% of special education students are physiologically unable to read at grade level. In addition, about another 5% of other children are transient, non-English-speaking, or developmentally delayed.[1] If the goal is literally unreachable—as 100% would be—then our classroom educators will justifiably dismiss it as political rhetoric unrelated to reality in the trenches.

On the other hand, a lower goal—say 60% or 70%—is a conscious, long-term policy decision that limits how students can learn, forces middle and high schools to operate with significant numbers of low-performing readers, and constricts how these students will function later in our society. This chapter spells out Kennewick's reasons for choosing 90%.

One practice that educators have used in the past in dealing with percentages is for a district or a state to selectively exclude children who will do poorly before calculating the percentage test results. Using this method, the percentage goal can be set high by not reporting the special education, developmentally delayed, non-English-speaking, transient, and/or slow/delayed readers. In the past there has been an unspoken agreement not to test, count, or report children who will do poorly. These silent subtractions from our denominator increase our percentages. The results make our district or our state look better. They tend to balance out some differences between schools with different student populations. These are the "fairness to the schools" arguments for making reductions to the denominator.

---

[1] According to the U.S. Department of Education, Office of Special Education Programs, approximately 10% of all students have disabilities. This fraction breaks down this way: 51.1% have specific learning disabilities (of which 80% are generally estimated to be reading disability), 20.8% have speech or language impairment, 11.6% are mentally retarded, 8.7% have serious emotional disturbances, 1.8% have multiple disabilities, 1.3% are hearing impaired, 1.2 have orthopedic impairment, 2.2% are physically "fragile," 1.2% have visual impairment, and .1% have brain trauma or autism. See *UDOE Data Analysis System*, 222.3e.gov/pubs/OSEP961nlRpt/ Chap1b.html.

Five Considerations for Choosing Third Grade as the Assessment Point

1. **Physiological**. Children's brains develop at different rates. At fourth grade, more children can process symbols and make necessary connections than at second grade. Later than second grade is better.

2. **System engagement.** Most improvement will occur just before assessment, just as most studying occurs just before finals. Assessment at the fourth grade engages the system of teachers, principals, students, and parents late. Assessment at the fourth grade means that fewer children will reach the goal than assessing at the third grade. Earlier than fourth grade is better.

3. **Content.** With maturity, a child is able to process more content each day. A typical first-grade day covers relatively few concepts. By comparison, a fourth-grade day covers much more. If the point of accountability is too late, the content gap between students who "get it" and those who don't will be too great. Earlier than fourth grade is better.

4. **Home differences**. Many children come to school with little or no literacy experience. Sometimes they are not even able to recognize the letters of the alphabet. Reading instruction at school is designed to compensate. The students have to catch up; but at some point, if they have not caught up, they reach a point of diminishing returns. This point occurs in second or third grade.

5. **Assessment.** Up through the middle part of second grade is too early to use most standardized bubble-sheet tests with any degree of confidence in their mechanical accuracy. Seven-year-olds have a hard time with the mechanical tasks of staying on the right line and counting to the right bubble without help. Third grade may be too early for the day-long, in-depth statewide tests which are typically administered at the fourth grade. Third grade may also be too early for testing higher level processing and thinking skills. However, it is not too early to test basic reading skills. By fourth grade, reading assessments typically test vocabulary, concept recognition, and multiple meanings—far more than basic reading skills.

However, if we allow tinkering with the denominator, when a reading gain is reported, no one can distinguish real gain from phantom gain. No one can distinguish an actual increase in the number of students at the standard from more students excluded from the denominator. Using all children in the denominator removes any incentive to selectively test students without eliminating the option of a teacher or administrator of not testing a student who may be demoralized by it.

The goal is most fairly reported and most easily understood when we take the number of students who score at or above the standard (the numerator) and divide it by all students (the denominator). Using a full denominator creates accountability for all children. A goal of 90% lets a school district accept accountability for all of its reachable students. The real issue remains one of "fairness to the students."

Of course, equity and access issues are real. A district may have a military base or a Native American reservation in its borders. It may have an influx of migrant farm workers' children three weeks before the May testing. Districts can acknowledge the problems posed by transient and non-English-speaking students by using a secondary percentage that excludes these groups from both the numerator and denominator. Thus, we can clearly disclose to our public how we are doing under both full and adjusted denominators.

2. **Which grade level should be the measurement point?**

A board can choose to measure reading levels at the end of the second, third, or fourth grade. Kennewick's choice is the third grade. In 1998, the Washington legislature set the measurement point at the end of fourth grade. They selected fourth grade because of educational reform legislation (HB1209) already being implemented that tests students at fourth, seventh, and tenth grades. Choosing a different grade impacts each of the "Five Considerations" outlined below.

3. **What year should the goal be achieved?**

Choosing the spring of four years hence creates a promise for this year's kindergartners. It creates a clear accountability deadline in everyone's future. An average district, starting in the 50% range can achieve a 90% average by the time kindergartners or first graders finish third grade, if it achieves a 10% increase at each grade level each year.

Despite our modest expectations of 5-10%, using full denominator reporting, Kennewick's third graders improved 15% the first year and 16% the second year. Districts starting at the 30-40% range should give themselves a couple more years.

4. What process should be used in setting the goal?

A goal set by a state legislature must go through the legislative process. If the legislature requires that districts set a goal, as it did in February 1998 in Washington State, the goal-setting process occurs within the district. Because of the magnitude of this decision, the board should use a process which intentionally involves all of the stakeholders.

> "Goals help an organization to focus attention on relevant issues, set standards, attract and retain employees, understand internal operations, understand the system's character, and provide boundaries for decision making."
>
> —J. M. Ivancevich, Andrew D. Szilagyi Jr., and Marc J. Wallace Jr., *Organizational Behavior and Performance* (Goodyear, 1997), 245.

The delicate part of this process is dealing with the gulf between current reading levels and perceptions held by parents and the community of current reading levels based on information disseminated by the schools. This information has often been obscure, couched in the confusing language of stanines and percentiles. Even if the language was decoded accurately, the information was still obscure because it was phrased in terms of average third graders, not in terms of average first, second, third, fourth, or fifth graders. Board members can serve for a decade without understandable information on current reading levels.

When the reading levels of our lowest 40% are understood, natural reactions are denial ("It can't possibly be this bad"), anger ("Why haven't we been told?"), and accusation ("What are you doing about it?"). It's best to handle these reactions proactively, with hard-edged easily understood figures and with absolute honesty. Specific reports at board meetings over a three-month period can systematically eliminate denial. Board reports can convert third- and fourth-grade reading percentiles to grade-level equivalents building by building to show the wide range in reading ability as well as the deficiencies of the lowest 25%. Reports can correlate the reading levels of sixth, seventh, and eighth graders with office referral for discipline (see Chapter 4) and can track the reading levels of high school dropouts.

It's also best to keep focused on the goal—a child who can read—and not get sidetracked into blaming games. The energy which comes from the heightened awareness can be directed positively by the district's setting of a reading goal. Even an angry reaction can be positive when the valuable energy it generates has a clear channel for helpful and cooperative action.

Stakeholders should be involved in the information-reporting process. They should be members of the various groups considering the alternative percentages, alternative years, alternative time periods, and awareness of the size of the task. Involving the community, teachers, and especially parents creates the ownership necessary for long-term support.

While virtually everyone has an interest in this issue, you should expect significant divergence in response. Business leaders, the media, parents, and students will ask why the 90% goal is being set so low. If it is set lower yet, they will ask why so many children are being intentionally left behind.

Ways of Saying What We Want

Some ways are more powerful than others. Some are more appropriate in a given district than others. Here are some ways to clearly state what we want:

- *Adopt the goal in a board resolution.*
- *Adopt the goal as a major objective in our strategic plan.*
- *Incorporate the goal in every other key district document.*

Ways of Not Saying What We Want

- *Funding a salary increase is not saying it.*
- *Reviewing the test scores is not saying it.*
- *Holding a workshop on reading is not saying it.*
- *Buying more books for a library is not saying it.*
- *Selecting a new reading approach is not saying it.*
- *Asking for improvement in reading is not saying it.*
- *Authorizing the purchase of a new reading series is not saying it.*

All of the items on this list are process activities and input activities. Focusing on process and inputs are all ways of not focusing on outputs and results.

Middle school and high school teachers and administrators will support any increase in reading ability.

Elementary principals may resist any measurable goal because inevitably their job evaluations will be linked to the effectiveness of their instructional leadership in reading.

The incubation period provided by the board agenda may eliminate surprises. Discussion, information, debate, examples, and evaluation, however, do not guarantee consensus. Ultimately, the board must act. We must say what we want. If we really want at least 90% of our children to read well, we must say so.

"For these are all our children and we will either benefit [them] or pay the consequences for whom they become."

—James Baldwin

If as boards and superintendents, we don't say what we want, we tacitly invite our state and federal legislators to say it for us. We have the same constituents. The same voters elect each of us. Parents want their children to read, and employers want their employees to read. If first graders could set the goal, where would they put it?

CHAPTER ELEVEN

TESTING AND STANDARDS

"If you cannot measure it, you cannot change it."

—Edwards Demming

Chapter 10 outlined the process of setting the reading percentage, determining the measurement point, and defining the time period in which to achieve it. The final issue is defining "at or above grade level." To establish a baseline and report progress toward our chosen goal in terms of children at or above a certain standard, we must (1) give a test which accurately measures student reading achievement, and (2) establish a fixed reading standard in relationship to the test. Washington's test and standard has already been selected on a state level, thus creating uniformity among its districts.

> *"Good testing results in better data to make better curriculum and instructional decisions. Better decisions result in greater student achievement."*
>
> —Allan Olson, Executive Director, Northwest Evaluation Association

Selecting the Test to Measure Reading

There are dozens of good basic reading tests available. We chose those of the Northwest Evaluation Association because of how precisely this organization's product matched our needs. (See "NWEA's Tests" at the end of this chapter.) As your district chooses its reading test, here are six issues to consider.

First, assessing elementary reading should be the first step in assessing student achievement in grades three through twelve. While your board is spending the money to assess elementary reading, it should consider how to make it part of a larger and integrated effort to assess students in core subjects in grades 3-12. In Kennewick, our reading goal grew out of a larger effort to establish grade-level assessments, grade-level standards, grade-level reports, and accountability. (See Appendix E, "The Kennewick Strategic Plan," Goals 2 and 3.) Using a commercially produced bank of test questions that cover grades 3-12 in reading, math, and science provides a sophisticated information management tool for student academic achievement. Often this is the first time this information has ever been available for the board. These tests can:

> *Once a state has set minimum standards at certain points, for example at grades four, seven, and ten, it is a natural and almost inevitable step for districts to create standards at each of the grades in between. Districts will next install measurement systems and begin reporting student achievement to parents in terms of these grade level standards and benchmarks.*

- Measure the progress from September to May (or May to May) of each student, each classroom, each building, and the district.
- Track the progress of each student from second through twelfth grade.

Second, consider selecting tests which can be machine-scored in the district. When test results are available within a few days or weeks, they have greater impact than results that are delayed three or four months.

Third, consider selecting a type of test which can be "renewed" or "refreshed." Teachers should be able to "teach to the test" but not "teach the test." When teachers repeatedly administer the same test, there is a natural and unconscious tendency to teach students the answers to the specific test questions during the year. This activity skews the test results. A test constructed from a test bank that has ten identically weighted and equally difficult, but differently worded, questions, can be "renewed" with minimal effect on the test by rotating the questions. For example, the question on two-digit addition on the math test can be exchanged for any one of the other ten equally difficult two-digit addition problems from the data bank, without affecting the comparability of the test results.

Fourth, consider choosing tests that can measure annual student growth. Tests that can be given in September and again in May engage students and teachers, because they measure individual student and individual teacher performance over a year. Tests which measure individual student growth along a continuum of grades 3-12 can be aggregated to track growth in a class, a school, and a district, by year and across years. Tests given at wide intervals (for example, the fourth, seventh, and tenth grades) are not very effective at measuring student growth. They do provide information about how students compare to other groups of students and measure curriculum effectiveness. Most state interval tests are normed tests and provide a comparison of a district's student performance against a national norm, thus allowing a district to compare its curriculum and instructional levels with those of districts throughout the country.

Fifth, consider tests which provide accurate grade-level equivalents from the lowest achieving students through the highest achieving students. Tests should not compress the range of low scores for the lowest achieving students into a single score at a higher grade-level equivalent. Compressed reporting of scores in this fashion gives our boards, legislators, parents, and communities the worst information about our most critical populations. (See Chapter 3.)

Sixth, consider testing in kindergarten, first, and second grade as well as testing in the third grade. Each year an increasing number of second graders must come to third grade reading at grade level if third grade teachers are to get their classes to 90%. Third-grade teachers cannot be expected to make 40% gains. More children must make more gains at kindergarten, first, and second grade. To assure greater uniform improvement at the lower grades, Kennewick is extending the Northwest Evaluation Association functional level testing to the second grade. The district is implementing the Test of Phonemic Awareness (TOPA), a teacher-based screening test, in kindergarten and tests of the other enabling skills appropriate for first grade. These are district-level decisions because they deal with assessment, not curriculum.

Screening kindergarten and first-grade students is a touchy area. These students are too young to take bubble tests without assistance. Every responsible K-1 teacher feels morally obligated to explain this fact to any board member who doesn't already know it. As additional assessment is introduced at earlier levels, teachers should actively participate in selecting the kind of tests to be used, and the reasons for selecting the tests should be clearly articulated.

These six issues should guide considerations in assessment selections. The cautions should be taken seriously, but the crucial advantage of tests is that they cut through "feeling good" and get to student achievement. Every test has limitations. But radar guns and breathalizer tests eliminate most of

NWEA's Tests

Over the past twenty-five years, NWEA has worked with trained educators to develop item banks of questions that are calibrated against an equal-interval scale (RIT scale). These items have been through an extensive review process and field tested to ensure appropriate validity and reliability measures. NWEA provides support to school districts to develop assessments that are aligned with local curriculums in reading, mathematics, language usage, and science. The NWEA Achievement Level Test system is an accurate tool for measuring student learning from second grade through high school. There is not a comparable assessment system that measures students' instructional level and growth from year to year.

NWEA item banks and software allow each district to develop a series of overlapping tests which together measure the reading learning continuum. The test series is not grade specific but rather measures each child's instructional level using a common achievement scale. This allows educators to use quality data to monitor student growth across years and to analyze the effectiveness of programs for individuals and groups of students.

Development of the Tests. NWEA provides an item bank of about 20,000 reading, language, mathematics, and science questions that are calibrated for difficulty using a common, equal-interval scale, the RIT scale. A team of teachers selected from the district develops tests for the elementary, middle, and high school programs using software provided by NWEA. The software ensures that each test covers the appropriate difficulty levels and goal structures, and that there is an equal distribution of items across the test range. NWEA controls the technical quality of every test.

Administering Achievement Level Tests. The tests themselves are 40-50 multiple-choice items with bubble answer sheets. They generally take about an hour, although they are not timed tests. Machine scoring takes place either at the NWEA office or at the local district, with a turn-around time of two weeks or less. Testing occurs at the beginning and end of each school year so teachers can monitor the progress of their students and analyze the effectiveness of their programs. Spring-to-fall test data can measure gains or losses made over the summer months.

NWEA's Tests

Teacher Buy-In to the Tests. When local teachers select the test questions, it becomes "our" test. The repetitive explanations offered by administrators year after year for the results of the national tests simply don't surface. We are testing "our" curriculum and in the order in which it should have already been taught. We are using instruction terms that are familiar to our children.

Standard Setting. NWEA Achievement Level Tests give a range of scores. When Kennewick started, the scores ranged from a low of 145 to a high of 244. NWEA provides a chart for converting the scores into grade-level equivalents. The grade-level equivalents at the beginning of each September identify where the average American child scores. The equivalents over the other eight months are then extrapolated, assuming that growth occurs in equal intervals during those eight months.

In the Kennewick School District, reading at or above grade level by the end of third grade is measured by achieving the score of 194 on the NWEA Achievement Level Tests in May of the third-grade year. The score of 194 equates to the score of an average third grader in December, (third grade/fourth month). The setting of this standard, like the setting of any standard, is a wholly arbitrary decision. There was a long internal debate where suggestions ranged from second grade/sixth month to third grade/ninth month.

Renewing the Test. Because there is a pool of several approximately equivalent questions for each needed test item, the test questions can be easily substituted from test to test, keeping the scoring and standards equivalent over years and between classes even when curriculum and programs change.

Conversion to Measurements of Central Tendency. Because the weight of the questions is correlated to national means, student scores can be compared on an individual, class, school, or district level to national means, medians, stanines, and percentiles. More importantly, the scores can be translated to grade-level equivalents that everyone can understand.

the factual disputes in speeding and DUI cases, and good tests eliminate most of the factual disputes in reading discussions. They are an absolutely essential part of reading accountability—necessary in assuring system growth over time. The judicious selection of a solid reading test permits the next step, which is to set the reading standard.

> "Our testing system has done great things for us. It is worth every penny we put into it."
>
> —Greg Fancher, Director of Elementary Education, Kennewick School District

Setting a Fixed Reading Standard

Here is Kennewick's standard in non-technical terms: Our reading standard is that our students can uniformly and easily read the material at their grade level. In more technical terms, our reading standard is 194 on the functional-level tests developed from the Northwest Evaluation Association data banks. A score of 194 equates to third grade/fourth month, or the reading level of the average third grader in December.

One way of balancing where the standard should be against where the standard can be sustained is by using "negative impact data." Negative impact data means how many students are not at a proposed standard. For example, 70% of the students in our districts may score below the proposed standard. In anticipating the public outcry, should the bar initially be set lower so more students can get over it?

Because textbooks are written at national average grade levels, it seems to make sense to set a fairly high reading standard (as Dr. Terry Bergeson, Washington State Superintendent of Public Instruction, and a group of twenty-five teachers did in June 1997), and then take political considerations into account in determining the percentage goal.

Setting the U.S. standard for third-grade reading is a logical task for the National School Board Association in conjunction with professional reading associations. Until that happens, however, districts, State Departments of Education, or legislators in each state must go through this process individually. Current grade-level data are the most reliable indicator we have.

CHAPTER TWELVE

REPORTING THE RESULTS

"I think we as teachers often try to soften the blow and not let parents know how far below grade level their child is reading and how it comes into play in all other subjects. Thank you for pushing us as teachers to be totally honest with parents. Hopefully, in return, parents will become more involved with their child's reading."

—Claudia Glover, reading specialist, Washington Elementary

When we communicate to our parents and public, we want to use terms they understand. When we report reading progress at the third (or fourth) grade, we report the percentage of students at or above the standard. Everyone understands a standard. Everyone understands below or above a standard.

And surprisingly, there are few questions about how the standard became the standard. Every industry sets standards, and no one is surprised that educators finally set one for reading.

In addition to knowing whether their child reached the standard, most parents want to know where in relationship to the standard their child is reading, as well as the amount of growth their child is making each year. This is especially true for children below the standard.

No member on our boards, newspaper editorial staff, or legislature can determine the number of students reading at a first- or second-grade level

The Normal Curve

Depending on the subject and the test, this range can represent anywhere from 4 - 8 years in grade level equivalents

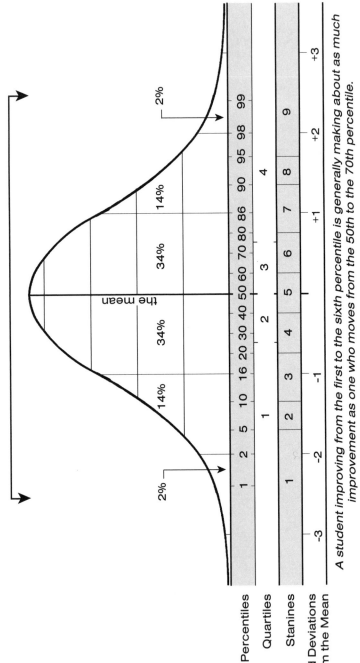

A student improving from the first to the sixth percentile is generally making about as much improvement as one who moves from the 50th to the 70th percentile.

by looking at our fourth grade reading scores reported in percentiles, stanines, quartiles, and standard deviations from the mean without the tests' conversion tables. And how many of us have ever seen those conversion tables? 10%? 2%? If that information is masked for us, it is masked for our parents as well.

The most common method of reporting test results has been based on statistical measures of central tendency graphically represented by the bell curve. The most common statistic is the average. Other statistics derived from this method are the median, percentile rank, quartile, and stanine.

This statistical model has always been more mathematically elegant and internally consistent, because it never involved the messy and arbitrary process of setting a fixed external standard. Large testing companies can independently develop, market, and score their tests without reference to anything but the median test score of the average student taking the test.

Using the median scores on these tests to measure student performance is much like measuring the level of the tides by putting a block of wood in the ocean without putting a mark on the shore. The median score and the block of wood float up and float down and there is never a baseline point from which to measure institutional improvement.

Grade-Level Equivalents

The easiest and most understandable way to think about standards is in terms of grade-level equivalents. Most reading tests generate a raw numerical score which can be converted to reading progress by year (like second, third, or fourth grade) and also by month. A perfectly "average" third grade child will get a numerical score in September which converts to "third grade/first month." If that perfectly "average" child continues to make normal improvement for the entire school year, he or she would get a numerical score on a test given the following May that would convert to "third grade/ninth month."

Typically the September numerical scores at each grade are carefully field-tested, but the months in between are extrapolated. It's something like a yardstick where the foot measurements are very precise, but the inch marks are approximate.

But the problem greater than the floating median is the inscrutable and unreferenced distance between the 1st and 50th percentile. No one can tell what a 1st or 10th or 20th percentile means without reference to an external measure, a grade-level equivalent.

Terms and Definitions for Extra Credit

The raw score is the number of right or wrong answers a student gets on a given test. In a test of 50 questions, before weighting, a student could get a low of zero and a high of fifty as a raw score.

The median is the selection of the raw score of the middle most student. If the raw scores of 100 students are grouped from high to low, the median score is the raw score of the 50th student.

The percentile ranking is a continuation of the median process. The lowest 1% of the scores is the first percentile. The next lowest percent is the second percentile. This process continues to the top 99 percent of the scores which is the 99th percentile. When a student scores in the 12th percentile, it means that 87% of other test takers scored higher. A lot of test design is based on selecting questions that create this top-to-bottom spread.

Quartiles are four equal groups of percentile rankings of 25 percentiles each. The top quartile is the students in the 75th to 100th percentile. The bottom quartile is the students in the 1st to 25th percentile.

Stanines are nine unequally sized groups of percentile rankings. Stanines 1 and 9 contain the lowest and highest scoring 4 percentiles. Stanines 2/8, 3/7, and 4/6 contain the next lowest and highest 7, 12, and 17 percentiles respectively. Stanine 5 contains the 20 percentiles between 40 and 50.

Reliability is the extent to which student scores may vary because of different kinds of measurement error instead of what students know. Examples are excessively small type size or difficulty in transferring answers to bubble scoring sheets which can occur for young children.

Grade-level equivalence is the translation of percentile ranking into grade-level achievement. A grade-level equivalent of 3.6 (GE 3.6) means that the student is doing as well as the average third-grader in the third grade sixth month.

Norm-based tests result in a lack of fixed standards and fixed standard reporting. In our opinion, this lack is directly responsible for the abysmal state of elementary reading. We have had decades of statistical reporting where the mid-point floated up and down, and few decision makers understood how far the end points were from that floating mid-point.

A criterion-referenced test is designed to test student progress toward understanding and applying specifically taught concepts. The reporting format uses the level of learned information or skill as the primary comparative basis.

A norm-referenced test is designed to measure differences among individuals composing the group. Those reports use other student scores as the primary basis of comparison. An important design criteria is the selection of questions which highlight differences among students. Because fixed external standards are inherently inconsistent with norm-reference methodology, statistical reports mask whether a third-grader's reading level is so low that it will interfere with the learning of academic content.

In contrast to norm-based tests, the greatest strength of criterion-referenced testing and setting fixed standards is how easy it becomes to identify students who are reading above and below the standard. The results are clear: A student is either at or above the standard, or is below the standard. Parents, teachers, and community members have accurate information from these reports. The district can immediately tell with complete confidence whether more or fewer students are reading at or above the standard over time.

Furthermore, in addition to reading, this type of assessment can be used with math, science, or social studies at each level. These tests provide comparability across schools and communities. The results are fairly difficult to distort or to mask.

When we create a mechanism for reporting reading achievement, we are creating part of an accountability system. The purposes of the reporting are (1) to be sure that people essential to meeting the goal become engaged with the process, and (2) to create direct accountability for teachers, administrators, and boards and indirect accountability for parents. Simple, accurate, and reproducible reporting at the state, district, building, and student level is necessary for achieving these two purposes.

Reporting by Grade-Level Standards

When a May reading standard is in place for kindergarten, first, and second grades, as well as third and fourth grades, districts, parents, and the community can map student scores against these standards.

Reporting by District

Reporting by district creates a stake in the reading results by the board and central administration. The goal is not merely a student or a building goal. It is a multi-level team effort. Reporting the number of students at or above the standard and dividing by the total number of students provides the community with a clear picture of reality.

Reporting by Building

The delivery system of reading is not the state, the district, or the classroom. It is the elementary school. It is the team of teachers and administrators who serve the kindergarten, first, second, and third grades in a building. It is highly unlikely that 90% of our children will read at grade level unless each elementary system functions as a team. The most powerful way to get buildings to function as a team is to report the results of their collective efforts. Reporting by school also lets schools get an objective evaluation of their own growth. The scores cause more exchange of ideas among principals because they see which schools have made significant gains.

Some districts resist reporting scores by schools. Until Kennewick's new reading focus, the district had not disclosed academic performance school by school for decades. The reasons for masking school names include:

- It creates competition between schools. Competition in education is assumed to be bad.
- It is unfair because it compares rich schools to poor schools. The implicit assumption is that rich schools will always do better than poor schools, because difficult socio-economic backgrounds actually cause poor reading.
- It exposes principals to criticism when their schools consistently score poorly.

Our districts must transcend these reasons if we hope for significant improvement at the building level. There are vast differences in the instructional delivery systems among schools. There is an enormous range in the percentage of students at or above the reading standard among schools with near-identical populations. Reporting by building quickly identifies effective and ineffective instructional deliveries in similar populations while allowing for the fact that stable, supportive families above the poverty level usually provide a superior reading-rich experience for their preschoolers.

If school anonymity has been part of the local culture, here are some reasonable accommodations that can be made:

- Publish the results internally for the first year to allow schools a year of initial improvement.
- Advise principals of this plan during the first testing cycle to reduce stress.
- Focus on incremental improvement as well as end results to create a more supportive environment. The baseline of each building is the result of years of teacher in-service, educational conferences, prior supervision, and prior educational philosophy. The expectation of consistent yearly growth toward the goal provides balance in building-by-building reporting.

Reporting by Class

In Kennewick, we do not yet report by class because we have considered the teaching team as a unit. Class information can be extracted from the information given to the buildings, however, and most teachers and principals in Kennewick scrutinize that information very carefully.

Reporting by Student

Testing capable of accurately measuring the full continuum of reading levels shows that Kennewick third graders read on eight different grade levels. An essential piece of the reading accountability mechanism is telling parents where on this eight-grade continuum their child reads. At the end of Kennewick parent-teacher conferences, parents walk out, not only with oral information, but also with their child's scores in writing and a copy of the conversion chart.

As board members, we need to be aware of the pressure and trauma created at this step. Teachers work hard to make parent conferences a positive time. Teachers want to report success. For children reading at or above grade level, transferring this information is reassuring and inspiring. Teachers like telling it. Parents like hearing it. But it's different when a child is below grade level, especially when the gap is significant. In the past, teachers tactfully but vaguely described children reading below grade level as "a little slow" or "needs to work a little harder" but "will catch up in a few years."

Although parents did not understand exactly what this meant, they felt reassured that things were basically all right. Now large numbers of parents will receive a message from their child's third-grade teacher something like this:

"It's November of Tony's third-grade year, but he's reading at a first grade / sixth month level. What this means is that after twenty-four months of formal schooling,[1] Tony is fifteen months behind."

> "Eyeball accountability today drives system change tomorrow."
>
> –Lynn Fielding, Kennewick School board

Although it is difficult to give this news and difficult to receive this news, it is a powerful part of the reporting mechanism. It creates "eyeball accountability" between every third-grade teacher and every parent in every building. Principals and elementary teachers don't like reporting failure, and parents don't like hearing it. But it's not a personal issue between them. Both parents and teacher care—and care intensely—about that child. The enemy is not the teacher, not the parent, but whatever is blocking Tony's reading. They are partners and allies. Shock and disappointment can be powerful motivations to join forces to tackle the problem. Together they will do whatever it takes to create success.

On a district level, "doing whatever it takes" quickly takes the form of alerting parents about reading problems as early as kindergarten. Once this happens, parents will insist on regular reports and ask how they can help. When teachers urge daily home-reading, more and more parents do it and do it willingly. Teachers have strong motivation to match individualized teaching techniques to individual reading needs. Their reward for relentless efforts to improve reading programs is the improvement itself.

---

[1] This calculation is based on a half-day kindergarten.

CHAPTER THIRTEEN

RESETTING DISTRICT PARAMETERS

"If we do not teach our children to read well by third grade, it rarely matters what else we do teach them."

—Paul Rosier, Superintendent, Kennewick School District

As boards and superintendents invite schools to make the changes necessary to reach a seemingly impossible goal, we should ease the restrictions, real or perceived, under which principals and their staff must function. One of the clearest ways to expand their parameters is in a position paper or, to use the British parliamentary term, a "White Paper." Unlike a board policy or regulation, a white paper allows broader input from educators and the community. It expresses a philosophy, articulates values, and defines expectations but in a flexible format that allows for developing competing ideas, dealing with problems, and updating.

This chapter quotes the seven parameters of Kennewick's Reading White Paper (boldface) and provides an extended commentary (roman).

1. **THE BUILDING-BY-BUILDING APPROACH: Primary planning and program change are to be on a building-by-building basis.**

When a board of education perceives a district-wide problem with the reading skills of its elementary-age students, it has a tendency to immediately find and impose a district-wide one-curriculum-size-fits-all solution. However, before we make the illogical leap that all our schools should use the same approach, we should consider these issues:

- First, accountability programs should be distinguished from instructional programs. The overall accountability system should be uniform across the district. It makes sense to have common district benchmarks, assessments, reporting, and sharing of strategies. But it is not equally reasonable to have district-wide instructional programs.

> *"We're not telling professional teachers how to teach—because only they can look into a child's eyes to see if the child understands. The teacher has the freedom to change his or her program until the look of understanding comes into that child's eyes. And that flexibility is the main ingredient of our success."*
>
> —Dan Mildon,
> Kennewick School Board

Most of the 15,000 districts in the U.S. have had a single district-wide instructional approach with the same curriculum being adopted district-wide. Our current state of reading may be the result of this single-bullet approach. Almost any single approach will reach 50%-60% of the children in the average classroom. However, each approach reaches a different 50-60%.

The Kennewick Reading White Paper: A Seven-Point Summary

1. **A BUILDING APPROACH:** Primary planning and program change will be on an elementary school-by-school basis.

2. **PLANNED, INCREMENTAL, AND CONTINUOUS GROWTH:** The district expects planned, incremental, and continuous improvement at kindergarten through third grade from each school's baseline to the goal over the next three years.

3. **PRIMARY ACCOUNTABILITY:** Primary accountability is with building principals.

4. **INCREASED RESOURCES:** Each elementary school should identify and alter decade-old paradigms that limit the existing resources that are spent on reading.

5. **CHANGES K-2:** Our primary approach is intervention at grades K-3, not remediation commencing in the fourth grade.

6. **RESULTS ORIENTED:** Programs will be evaluated on the basis of whether they work.

7. **EXPECTATIONS:** We expect all children, including those from low socioeconomic backgrounds, to reach the reading goal.

Teachers need to use seven to ten different teaching strategies to reach all of their children. By the time teachers are targeting the last three children in their classes who are not reaching the grade-level standard, they must reach deeply into their repertoire to match technique against need. A single district-wide approach discourages the development of the very repertoire necessary to reach the goal.

"Research also indicates that different children come to school with different levels of reading preparation and that they master the skills of reading at different rates. Thus, adopting one uniform teaching method for all children from varying levels of preparation does not yield the best results for the greatest number of children. Additionally, even with strong, research-based instruction, a small number of students will still face problems due to learning disabilities or other difficulties; these children will need carefully tailored tutoring and remediation."

—James Kilpatrick, Former Director of Policy Development for the U.S. House of Representatives Education and Workforce Committee

- Second, the logical extension of selecting a single instructional approach is to keep bumping the decision higher until finally each state's Department of Education prescribes the instructional program. We all know that doesn't work.

Most boards and superintendents are very emphatic that the state has the right and responsibility to define goals and standards, but they want to be free to determine how to reach these goals in a way that is compatible with local conditions and demands. It is only fair to give individual principals the same flexibility that we superintendents and boards ask from our states. We should tell elementary schools what we want and then give them the freedom to determine how best to do it.

- Third, when central administration (or the state) selects a single instructional program, the building's job is to implement that program and provide paperwork demonstrating its thorough compliance. This replaces the goal of actually teaching the children. The principal's job is clear: to implement the process as flawlessly as possible. But the responsibility for getting 90% of children to the goal has shifted to central administration (or to the state). Central administration models and state-wide models have not worked in the past.

2. **PLANNED, INCREMENTAL, AND CONTINUOUS IMPROVE-MENT:** Each school is starting from a different place with different levels of incoming students, different parent support, different expertise, and different effectiveness. The district expectation is for significant continuous progress at each grade level. It expects that each building will develop a plan, based on its population and reading levels, for immediate implementation within existing resources. Some schools will reach and maintain the goal more quickly than other schools. Some schools will have immense difficulty reaching the goal within three years. The district expectation is that significant, measurable progress will be evident each spring on the functional-level reading tests.

The district expects each school to make planned, continual progress over time from its baseline until it reaches its goal. Schools should not merely plan "to improve." That's a "feel good" process. Planned, incremental, and continual improvement to a goal is a quantifiable, accountable process that produces significant program innovation. The recurring criterion in planning to reach the goal is whether change in an activity, program, curriculum, etc., is deep and profound enough to increase the number of students reading above the minimum standard.

"This is my tenth year as an elementary principal. The job has always been an exciting adventure. But the last three years with the 90% reading goal have created what I can best describe as a pressured excitement that can be felt throughout the school. I feel new commitment from all realms—staff, parents, and students.

This excitement has three aspects. First, the reading goal provides a focus for all of the elementary schools in Kennewick. Second, this goal is measurable. Growth toward the goal is a celebrated event. And third, our school board set the goal and is definitely behind it, but each elementary building is allowed to choose and use the methods that work best for that building. Accountability, coupled with autonomy and support, is an excellent combination for success."

—Terry Tannenberg, Principal, Sunset View Elementary

Because of the building-level focus, the board doesn't usually get involved in planning; but it helps create deadlines by scheduling workshops in which each school presents its plans. Kennewick holds these reading workshops, one per board meeting, generally twice a month during the school year. If these workshops become numerically unwieldy in larger school districts, then dividing board members and central office personnel into smaller groups would limit each board member involvement to seven to ten workshops.

It has been our experience that elementary schools rarely have these kinds of workshops with their boards. As a result, they have been extraordinarily well-prepared and extraordinarily sensitive to board comments as well.

In Kennewick, an elementary school's reading workshop is typically held as a board meeting with a workshop session at the school. (See Chapter 7.) Most of the school's personnel attend. After the board attends to any district business (5-8 minutes), the workshop is turned over to the building principal who introduces the staff, provides a program overview, and introduces the next presenter. Generally, a teacher at each grade level presents aspects of that grade's reading process.

The style, energy, and level of cooperation of each staff member quickly become apparent, as does the management and leadership style of each principal. The personality and energy of each staff directly impacts their joint ability to maximize each other's strengths in creating fairly complex reading strategies and social structures to teach different student populations. Some staffs are tense, closed, fragmented, and resistant to uniform solutions. Even one toxic individual diminishes the performance of the school and rapidly becomes a liability that other faculty become less willing to tolerate.

However, we have found that most staffs tend toward high competence, openness, risking, and willingness to team. A measure of morale is that 80-90% of the entire elementary school's staff typically attended each workshop, highly prepared and enthusiastic. We liked what we were seeing.

—Ed Frost, Kennewick School Board

These meetings are an absolutely essential time for positive and supportive comments that reinforce the expectation of a shared team effort and progress over time.

The power of the workshops was enhanced during the first year when the board and superintendent decided it would be useful to circulate the minutes and some of the handouts of these first-year workshops to every elementary school in the district. The minutes created an immediate sense of movement and energy. Because there is surprisingly little communication among elementary buildings in medium- and large-sized districts, these minutes shared what is working.

Our first workshops were with highly successful buildings that modeled innovation and effectiveness. Making supportive and positive

The School Board's Reading Workshops:
A Teacher's Perspective
Steve Linn
Lincoln Elementary, Third Grade

When our school presented its workshop on reading for the board, the biggest benefit was that we teachers could see and celebrate our success. After an entire year of planning, implementing, and refining our reading strategies, we were amazed at what we had really achieved.

Yes, we'd all worked at raising the literacy level in our classrooms, concentrating on fitting teaching to our students' different cognitive and developmental levels. But in the presentation, we saw the bigger picture. We could see that progress was being made. Reading ability across the school had risen in spite of different tools, personalities, and methods.

As a result, we've been able to dovetail each succeeding grade level's plans into the preceding one. It helped us be on the same page with our colleagues. Looking critically at what we were doing brought unity, a sense of accomplishment and validation, a celebration, and renewed energy for the next year.

When the school board visited our school, watching our strategies and materials in action, it let us know that the board members were involved on a much deeper level than just throwing us a goal. Their visit said volumes about being in this venture with us. We felt supported and encouraged. While we teachers may be in the foxholes, the board was willing to check the front lines for victories, casualties, and the need for reinforcements.

We appreciated their probing questions. When we told them candidly that disintegrating family structures were sending our students to school with encumbering issues that made it hard to meet our goal, there was no blaming or phony pep talks. One member simply asked, "What can we do on a practical level that would help?" It was a great interchange. It's easy to press forward, knowing you're listened to and supported.

comments was easy and set an optimistic tone throughout the district. Typically, presenters from these schools emphasized the importance of leadership from their principals, an important message to highlight in the minutes.

3. **PRIMARY ACCOUNTABILITY: Primary accountability is with building principals. Elementary principals will be expected to provide significant leadership to achieve this goal, including reprioritizing existing activities. Because building principals do not teach reading, they should view their role as supporting those who do. An increasing portion of elementary principals' annual evaluations will result from the district's professional appraisal of effective leadership in this area.**

Only principals can create the school-level teams necessary to assure that children uniformly reach the reading goal. As teachers left basal reading series (the more regimented reading textbook series used nearly universally until the late 1970s), the structure that these textbooks gave reading programs between grade levels gradually dissipated. Teachers became independent reading providers. As the competition between proponents of whole language and phonetics became more intense, teachers tended to withdraw, close their doors, and teach within their comfort zones. Principals can create the teams that open the doors, keep ideas flowing, and pool urgently needed resources.

While we need to give principals flexibility and hold them accountable for the results, we need to do it gently and with support. The focus on accountability is coming down on principals nationwide. As we create systems of reading accountability, we should also create a supportive environment with many paths of formal and informal communication with our principals. Our experience has been that our principals welcome high expectations as long as the level of support and level of contact are also high.

4. **INCREASED RESOURCES: Decade-old paradigms have limited the resources spent on reading. Each building should identify and alter old and limiting assumptions. Paradigm shifts redirecting more resources to reading which have been suggested within the district to date include:**

a. More time. An extremely effective method of reading improvement is simply to spend more time on it. This common-sense notion is supported by research and also allows immediate action within existing budget constraints. Each K-3 teacher will be asked to evaluate the amount of time spent on reading. Elementary teachers have permission to expand the time spent on reading and cut the time spent on other areas immediately.

In Kennewick, we boldly speculated about letting K-3 teachers double the amount of time they spend on reading. What if we let them allocate whatever time they needed by whatever combination of people they decided? It would be a way of doubling or tripling the reading resources at virtually no additional cost. Research findings suggest that students have at least 2.5 hours of reading instruction in grade 1 and at least two hours in grades 2-5.

> When we double or triple the time or resources on reading by cutting other curriculum, the only cost is the lost curriculum itself. That loss is generally small for children who can read very little of it anyway.
>
> If the loss also occurs for children who can read, then calculating the loss becomes trickier as we try to offset short-term loss against potential increased gain as fourth-grade and fifth-grade classes move together and move faster.

b. More people. Ways to increase the people involved in reading at the school site include the use of student peers, the use of fourth and fifth graders with K-3 graders, the use of high school students at the elementary schools, and the expansion of parents and community volunteers.

c. More effective programs: K-3 teachers will be asked to identify and evaluate their current instructional techniques. Effective commercial programs should be evaluated. How effectively are we using reading specialists, Title 1 reading teachers, and special education staff?

"More effective reading programs" encourage the exploration of:

• Sending faculty to innovative seminars

• Experimenting with commercial programs

• Providing comparisons of different programs

• Targeting the most at-risk children with direct instruction like Distar.[1] Such programs are highly structured and repetitive. They are nowhere near as much fun for the adults, but they move struggling children slowly but successfully to readership.

d. More effective structural organization. Schools have permission to restructure the K-3 program.

"More effective structural organization" can take a variety of forms:

• Read in the mornings when students are fresh.

---

[1] Distar™ is a very structured step-by-step instructional program that has been extremely effective for children with reading skills below grade level.

- Use reading specialists exclusively at K-3.
- Use every available adult, including music teachers, PE specialists, and custodians for small-group reading every day.
- Assign homework requiring that the child read or have material read to him or her twenty minutes every day. Report progress on this homework on the report card.
- Use small-group, skill-based instruction for targeted needs.

e. More money: We plan to request as much as a half million dollars of increased funding in the levy in February 1996 (not available until April 1997).

When we asked schools to double their reading output, the first and burning question asked by principals was, "What happens on the input side?" The easy answer is always more new money. It has been the easy answer for the last two decades. Our goal moved us past the easy answer very quickly. There is very little new money. Even when there is new money, it typically doesn't amount to more than $40-$80 per elementary child per year versus the $6,000 average cost per child currently spent.

Inservice training for teachers in more effective techniques is one of the most effective places to put money.[2] Adding instructional methods targeted toward the slower reading populations is another. Proposing levies and earmarking increases specifically for reading makes an additional statement that the board is "putting their money where their mouth is." In Kennewick, we made all of our first year's gain without any new money from levies, thanks to our enormously creative and committed teachers and to the willingness of our administrators to shift existing resources.

Our Reading White Paper was an invitation for elementary schools to alter the rules. Another effect was to create more security for change. If a board wants to encourage more dramatic action, it has an accompanying responsibility to decrease the perceived disadvantages and reduce the risks involved. Decreasing the downside does not insure that faculty and administrators will, in fact, willingly take risks. But when those who must do the work—teachers and support staff—are debating alternatives in faculty meetings, those who do not want to change the curriculum have one less argument with which to oppose those who do.

---

[2] Dennis Sparks, "Interview with Robert Slavin," *Journal of Staff Development*, Spring 1998, 44-45.

5. CHANGES K-2: The summative evaluation at the end of the third grade is designed primarily for feedback for the K-3 process and not for remediation commencing in the fourth grade. Changes in the K-2 processes should include:

a. Specific kindergarten expectations and increased reading activities in grades 1-2.

b. Some kind of K, 1, and 2 testing so that teachers and principals can monitor the process early.

Move Fast, Intervene Early

- *Deferring intervention until third or fourth grade should be avoided at all costs.* [3]

- *Children with poor instruction in the first year are seriously harmed and do more poorly across the years.* [4]

- *Children who struggle unsuccessfully with reading in kindergarten and the first grade generally decide that they neither like nor want to read.* [5]

- *Seventy-five percent of first graders who had been in the bottom 10th percentile in phonological skills in kindergarten [in one year] moved to national averages in decoding with 20 minutes a day of one-on-one tutoring and practice in reading and writing.* [6]

Because improvement occurs immediately before the point of assessment, it is essential that second-grade, first-grade, and kindergarten teachers be engaged. If they are not, then other districts will have the same problem Kennewick saw: vast improvement in reading scores between the beginning and end of third grade but virtually no increase in the number of children reading at grade level when they enter third grade.

---

[3] Catherine E. Snow, M. Susan Burns, and Peg Griffin, eds., *Preventing Reading Difficulties in Young Children* (Washington, DC: National Research Council/National Academy Press, 1998), 326.

[4] R. C. Pianta, "Widening the Debate on Education Reform: Prevention as a Viable Alternative," *Exceptional Children* 45, no. 4 (1990): 306-13.

[5] C. Juel, "Learning to Read and Write: A Longitudinal Study of 54 Children from First through Fourth Grades," *Journal of Educational Psychology* 80, no. 4 (1988): 437-47.

[6] J. K. Torgesen, R. K. Wagener, and C. A. Rashotte, "Preventing and Remediating Severe Reading Disabilities: Keeping the End in Mind," *Scientific Studies of Reading* 1 (1997): 217-34.

6. **RESULTS, ORIENTATION, AND DISTRICT SUPPORT: The district is not adopting a model or theory. Districtwide adoptions in the past have resulted in our current reading levels and will likely only maintain them in the future. The district's primary effort will be to support building programs and actions which appear reasonably calculated to achieve the third-grade summative reading goal.**

> "We will find a way or we will make a way."
>
> —Hannibal on crossing the Alps

Kennewick's standard for evaluating the effectiveness of any reading proposal is one question: "Does it work?" A board or a legislature slides away from accountability and spirals down into process when it gets into how reading is taught. Debating techniques is a way of avoiding a concentration on results. No parent, director, or legislator will be happy with a program that is not working regardless of its pedigree or fashionableness.

7. **EXPECTATIONS FOR STUDENT PERFORMANCE: We get what we expect. Effective programs with low socioeconomic children are characterized by overt structure and high expectations. Our instructional strategies should focus on structural approaches that match a school's student body.**

Low Income, Poor Readers?

- *The correlation between SES [socioeconomic status] and achievement scores is low when measured individually. It is much higher when large numbers of these students attend the same school.*[7]

- *Low SES students progress at identical rates as middle and high SES students during the school year, but they lose ground during the summer.*[8]

Kennewick's superintendent and board have been pretty blunt on this point. One of the most disconcerting experiences for many of us was of growing up poor, working hard to get a good education, becoming financially independent, returning to education to "pay back" what we received, and hearing that we can't expect certain schools to teach reading effectively because those schools are made up of children whose parents have the same socioeconomic background that we had.

---

[7] K. R. White, qtd. in Catherine E. Snow, M. Susan Burns, and Peg Griffin, eds., *Preventing Reading Difficulties in Young Children* (Washington, DC: National Research Council/National Academy Press, 1998), 126-27.

[8] K. Alexander and D. Entwisle, "Schools and Children at Risk," in *Family-School Links: How Do They Affect Educational Outcomes?* edited by A. Booth and J. Dunn (Hillsdale, NJ: Erlbaum, 1996), qtd. in ibid., 127.

Because of the pervasive economic research and educators' noncritical acceptance that economic correlation is the same as causation, your board can absolutely expect to be told that schools serving poor neighborhoods should not be expected to meet the reading goal. Board members should be ready to point out the large swings in scores between similarly situated schools in their own district as well as the research showing the effect of expectation on results.

Generations of Poverty?

"Many social analysts assume that the poor families live in cities and engender generation after generation of poverty. Research belies this stereotype. . . . Of families in the top or bottom 20% of income [in 1969], only about half remained in these classifications in 1978. Between 1969 and 1978, 25% of the families fell below the official poverty line in at least one year, but less than 3% remained below in 8 of the 10 years. Even these persistently poor defied stereotypes: two thirds lived in Southern states; one third were elderly; and only a fifth lived in large cities. Level of education was a minor influence in determining changes in wealth or poverty. Most decisive were voluntary changes in family structure—marriage or divorce, a birth, or a child leaving home. Job-related changes such as layoffs, and physical disabilities were second in importance."

—Herbert J. Walber and Arthur J. Reynolds [9]

The Kennewick experience shows that sustained board and superintendent expectations help principals and staff in making necessary instruction program changes. We refused to allow staff at workshops to use family economics as a justification for students who are not learning to read. The result was that all of the schools made and maintained substantial growth. Vista Elementary School, with a free- and reduced-lunch population of 39% of the students, was one of our two schools in 1998 to achieve the 90% goal.

John Stuart Mill said it best: "One person who has a belief is equal to 99 persons who have only interest."

---

[9] Herbert J. Walber and Arthur J. Reynolds, "Longitudinal Evaluation of Program Effectiveness," in *Yearbook of Early Childhood Education, Vol. 7*, edited by Bernard Spodek and Olivia N. Saracho (New York: Teachers College Press/Columbia University, 1997), 29-30.

CHAPTER FOURTEEN

Establishing Your Reading Foundation

"The Pasco School District is proud to be a charter member of the Reading Foundation. Literacy is the critical element behind everything that happens in a child's education. The foundation serves as a catalyst in our community for riveting public attention on the fact that it really does take a whole village to help our children grow. The future of education lies in forging strong partnerships with the world around us, and the Reading Foundation serves as a model for making a profound impact in this arena."

— Dr. George Murdock, Superintendent, Pasco School District

One of the purposes of the Reading Foundation is to advocate that reading aloud with children from birth through elementary school is an essential parenting practice. We want to add to our common beliefs and practices the concept that good parents spend at least twenty happy minutes a day in literacy-related experiences with their children. Research, repetitive teacher comments, and common sense indicate that this practice significantly aids our schools in attaining the 90% reading goal while tying families and communities closer together.

This chapter will walk you through the three main steps in establishing a reading foundation: formation, funding, and operation.

Formation

Literacy organizations already exist in your community. Here is why you might start a new one rather than affiliating with an existing one. A new organization has no history and no baggage. It starts fresh. It has a single distinct message. The structure of the Reading Foundation, with districts as dues-paying members, creates a unique partnership between the community and school districts.

> We use of the word "Foundation" in our name to convey the size and scope of our mission. We are the "Reading Foundation" because every child needs a solid foundation in reading to succeed in life.
>
> —Nancy Kerr, President,
> the Reading Foundation

Most school districts, at the outset, are uncomfortable telling parents to read with their children. The community flavor of the foundation provides them with the slight distance that they prefer. A separate entity eliminates turf wars among competitive school districts and eliminates the kind of turf issues that sometimes occur when a mayor's office tries to create a school/community coalition from existing literacy groups, preschools, and school districts.

When ample support comes from school board members and superintendents, it assures that the foundation doesn't find itself in an adversarial relationship with the schools. It creates balance between school districts and community interests which is essential to achieving the 90% reading goal.

We suggest that this organization take the form of a nonprofit corporation organized under local state law. Consult an attorney. Two or three incorporators must be identified for legal purposes; they are members of the initial steering

The Reading Foundation's Vision of Success

Parents, as their child's first and most important teacher, read aloud with their children at least 20 minutes each day from birth.

Schools are committed and teaching to the high standard of children learning to read well and independently by the completion of third grade.

The entire community is organized and working together to ensure that all children acquire the fundamental reading skill necessary for success in school and life.

committee. They then adopt by-laws, outline a committee structure adopted to its purpose, appoint an interim president and executive director, and begin selecting the other nine to fifteen members of the board.

We suggest that these board members be members of the community who share three characteristics: (1) They provide immediate credibility for the foundation with the constituencies from which they are drawn, (2) They have the competency to make things happen immediately in a personal area of expertise (media, institutional access, fund raising, etc.), and (3) They are passionate about the specific, focused mission of the foundation.

Our board was strong and committed. They opened doors for us. They encouraged us. They did not micro-manage or see the foundation as a platform for launching other pet causes. Because the directors are highly visible and sit on numerous other community or business boards, they generally knew each other and were fairly sophisticated in how nonprofit organizations should run.

> *"Thanks to the tremendous support of our board of directors, community partners, schools, and families, the Reading Foundation has quickly grown from a few concerned citizens to an active organization mobilizing community resources to ensure that every parent has the information and support needed to raise a reader."*
>
> —Erin Tomlinson, Executive Director, the Reading Foundation

After its creation and at some point before the end of the first year, the organization's attorney should apply for tax-exempt status under Section 501(c)(3) of the Internal Revenue Code.

A lot of energy and money can be consumed in the start-up activities without much to show for it. This energy and money is better directed toward assuring that parents read with their children.

We're offering to help streamline the process for you. We have developed a "Reading Foundation in a Box" which explains how to replicate a chapter of this organization in your area, including (1) how to use existing organization formats, (2) funding concepts, and (3) many of the public relations and media tools we either developed or located.

Funding

Our Reading Foundation was initially funded by a membership fee of one dollar per student per district, contributed by the five school districts who first joined (now by ten districts). This funding provides the hard dollars for fixed costs like the salary of the half-to-three-quarters'-time executive director, telephone bills, printing, etc.

We did not want to become a fund-raising organization. That activity could consume a major portion of our time and energy. We saw our important work as involving others in ways that the message became their own.

And we saw it happen over and over: Our partners caught the vision. They promoted the reading message, represented it, and were original and authentic.

"Reading Foundation in a Box"

The "Reading Foundation in a Box" facilitates initial formation by providing copies of typical local incorporation, by-laws, and model 501(c)(3) applications. The tax exempt status application, which could cost $3,000 to $4,000 under normal circumstances, will cost about $1,000 using model applications forms. The initial first-year committee structure and proposed activities also help legitimize the organization by "quick and quality delivery" of an effective message.

The single prerequisite is that the initial incorporators include a school board member and a superintendent who have publicly committed to a reading goal and have involved community members with a track record of getting things done. A board member, a superintendent, and three community members make a good mix.

The media materials can be reformatted and distributed in your area with your local organization's tag line. The materials will allow you to create your own separate entity to promote the concept that parents and siblings read with children twenty minutes a day from birth. They will also show how to affiliate with the National Reading Foundation.

> To review these materials, visit website http:// www.readingfoundation.org. Use of these materials is unrestricted. The name is protected and can be used by becoming an affiliate of the National Reading Foundation.

Soft dollar contributions typically fund most of the projects and media coverage. For example, when the Harlem Globetrotters visit a community, they select a local organization to partner with to publicize their events. In 1997 in Kennewick, it was the Reading Foundation. Students who had read twenty minutes a day with their parents for the prior month were rewarded by a special "Globetrotter Pre-Event." The foundation paid air travel and lodging, contributed by a local business, for the two players who came. Kennewick police officers made up the exhibition teams. Schools organized the assemblies. Kennewick School District planned an evening event; four thousand kids and parents attended.

For the ratio of soft to hard dollars, the Reading Foundation spent about eight hundred hard dollars to pay its executive director to organize the event, locate and assure publicity for the supporting business, and "fine-tune" the message. The business contribution was about $2,400; the media contributed about $8,000 in free coverage, and the schools contributed the use of their buildings.

Our experience shows that, over the course of a year, the ratio of soft contributions to "hard" school contributions is about ten to one. For each dollar contributed by the school districts, the foundation received about three dollars of free media coverage, a dollar in business donations, and about six dollars of time and materials from clubs and organizations.

In addition, that same hard dollar generates hours of additional parent volunteer time that we can hang a price tag on.

> *"Our district's two primary goals for this school year are to help children build a solid foundation of reading skills and to multiply many times the number of parents and other caring adults who listen and read to children. We're pleased to know that we can count on the Reading Foundation to support our efforts with a lot of great ideas. We know that reading is the basis of all learning—and besides that, it's a great way to develop a relationship with young people that says, `I care about you.'"*
>
> —Dr. Otis A. Falls, Superintendent, North Franklin School District

We estimate a 24-35% increase in parent/child reading time in some districts. If a 30% increase in parents reading with children ages 0-8 occurs in a community with an investment of $1 per K-12 student, then each dollar generates 23 hours of additional "soft" contribution to children.[1] If the value of this reading time is computed at $15.00 per hour or $5.00 per day (which is far below the actual cost of delivering this service in any other way), every school dollar returns an additional $345 of literacy exposure.

Operations

The Reading Foundation's operational parameters have been to hire trusted people with a passion for the message and to stay out of their way. For our foundation, this is the executive director, who has also hired several project managers. We were particularly fortunate that Erin Tomlinson, our executive director, has a university degree in nonprofit business manage-

---

[1] For example, assume a community with 1,000 children at each grade level, making 13,000 students K-12. The Reading Foundation dues would be $13,000.

That community will also have about 8,500 children in the birth-through-third-grade bracket. It will take 121.6 hours per child per year to read to each twenty minutes. (365 days x 20 minutes a day per year = 7300 minutes divided by 60 minutes per hour = 121.6 hours per child per year.)

If there is a 30% increase in the time spent reading to 8,500 students, the annual school district investment of $13,000 will result in 310,000 additional hours of volunteer tutoring. That is 23.8 hours of additional volunteer time generated for each dollar of school district dues. (30% x 8500 students x 121.6 hours = 310,080 hours divided by $13,000 = 23.8 volunteer hours per school dues dollar.)

ment and had previously worked for the American Heart Association and United Way—but we really hired her for her fire and energy. We have generally limited our oversight to

- Budget review
- The reminder that this is a part-time job
- Suggestions about using the hard dollars to leverage community activities

Right from the start, the challenge for new foundations will be choosing which of the many worthwhile projects to pursue. There will be more possibilities than time to accomplish them. Therefore, it is valuable to prepare a simple strategic plan based on the goals of the Reading Foundation:

- Managing a long-term media/community education campaign to emphasize the importance of parenting and to encourage parents to read with their children twenty minutes each day.

Your Foundation Leaders

Finding the right president and executive director cannot be overemphasized. Your foundation needs leaders with superior social and political skills who can attract, coordinate, and graciously express appreciation for the contributions of diverse segments of your community. The organization and politics are complex, yet the "Read to Me" message is simple. Keep it simple. Resist hiring a reading expert whose vast knowledge will unintentionally complicate the message. There are already capable reading specialists in every school. Hire foundation leaders who are energetic organizers, visionary risk-takers, and true believers in the mission. It helps to have a president who is well connected and trusted in the community.

- Leading community-based activities and volunteer programs to ensure that all segments of our population demonstrate these values.
- Developing a clearinghouse of information and activities to support the involvement of others in literacy activities.

Under each goal, identify and prioritize important subgoals and activities (success indicators). Putting it in writing creates a map that guides you in making wise and leveraged decisions with confidence. Before we took this step, it was very stressful and confusing trying to respond to hundreds of great ideas.

For example, we determined to begin by "picking the low-hanging fruit first." We orchestrated a public awareness campaign aimed at parents who were most likely to read to their children. We prepared public service announcements for radio and TV, printed materials including a brochure, and distributed "Kids Who Read Succeed" buttons. We established relationships and shared our message with other community agencies that serve families, including over a thousand daycare providers. The Reading Foundation slogan, "The most important 20 minutes of your day . . . read with your child," permeated the local culture on reader boards, baseball and police trading cards, city signs, billing inserts, public service announcements, and bumper stickers. We asked schools to add reading reminders to all their communications with parents and to implement "20 minutes a day" or "100 minutes a week" as reading homework. Parents were hearing our message from many sources.

We followed our plan but also stayed spontaneous and willing to encourage others to sponsor activities that supported our goal. We were simultaneously implementing other important subgoals. Due to the enthusiastic and unexpected number of community-initiated service projects, our Reading Foundation accomplished its first five-year plan in a year and a half!

By generating a clear and continuous literacy message and by establishing connections between all members of the community, the Reading Foundation supports its member school districts' reading goals. When Erin Tomlinson speaks to community groups, she frequently tells this story to illustrate the Reading Foundation's mission:

"When I was growing up, Mom and Dad, who were both teachers, were very loving and intelligent parents; but they never required us to wear seat belts in the car. Nobody did. People just didn't understand the value of seat belts. Now, after twenty-five years of an ongoing public awareness campaign, I would never dream of moving my car until my daughter Abby is securely buckled up.

"I see the Reading Foundation creating a continual message in our communities about the importance of reading aloud with children every day. Parents are learning that this simple activity is vital to the well-being and success of their children in the twenty-first century. Most parents today will not drive without protecting their children. Tomorrow, most parents will not put their children to bed at night if the day has not included reading aloud together for twenty minutes."

> "It's important that your foundation hit the ground running. You'll get immediate credibility by offering obviously needed services—like READ*WRITE*NOW summer reading programs and effective media messages like the spots sponsored by the American Library Association that can be aired during Saturday morning cartoon shows."
>
> —Deb Bowen, Adjunct Lecturer/Marketing, Washington State University—Tri-Cities, and former Executive Director of the Reading Foundation

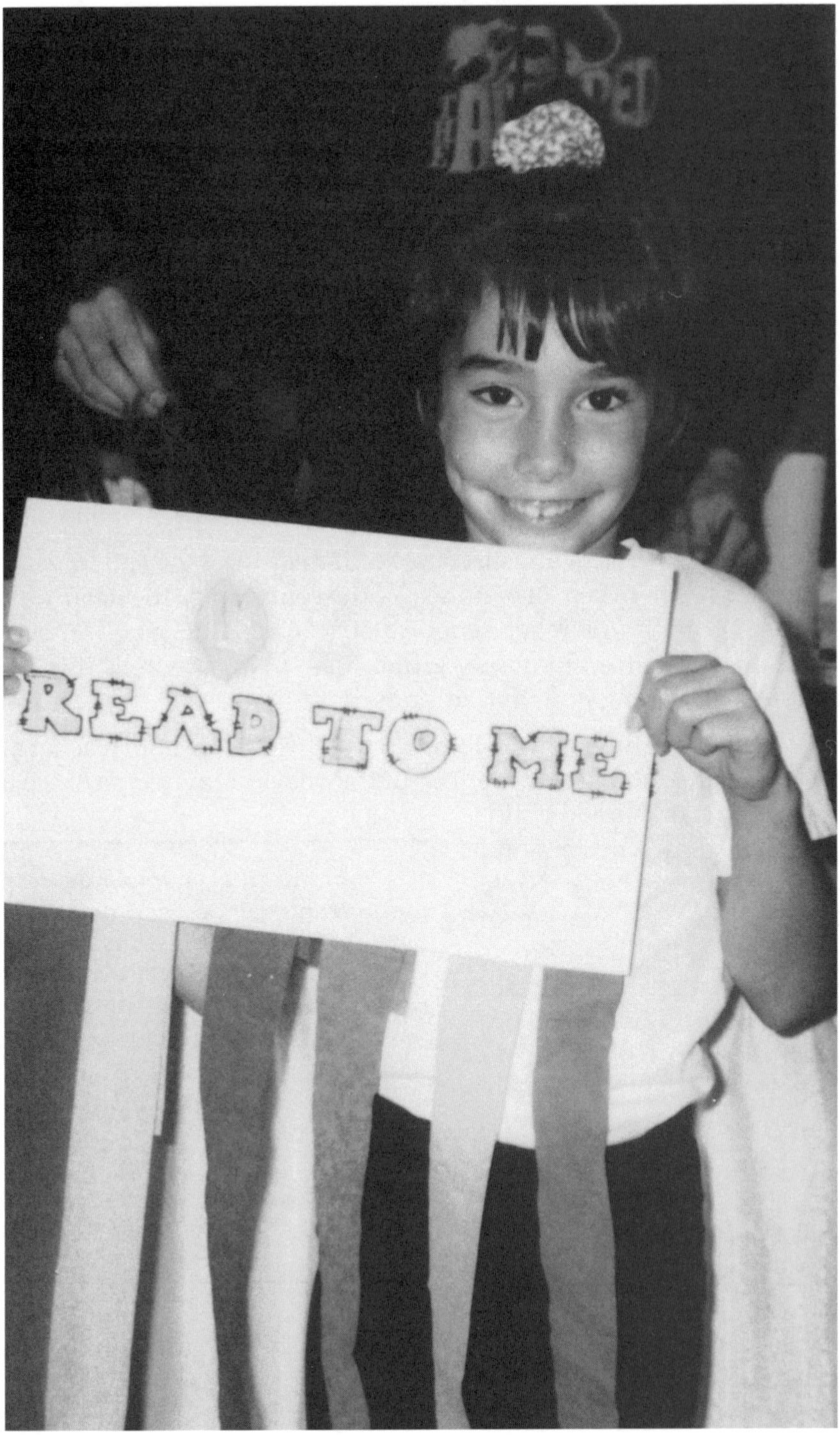
READ TO ME

EXTENDING ACCOUNTABILITY

Literacy accountablity must extend to our teacher colleges and from our state legislatures to each of our districts. Universities must assure that candidates for elementary teaching degrees are competent in teaching children to read. State legislatures must establish the assessments, standards, reports and institutional structures to assure that children read well in all school districts.

Part 3 describes how to prepare teachers and how to create state-wide reading accountability. It covers:

- •What Teacher Colleges Can Do (Chapter 15)
- •What Legislators Can Do (Chapters 16)
- •And What You Can Do (Chapter 17)

At 300 words a minute, the reading time for this part is 15 minutes.

What Teacher Colleges Can Do

"Today, an education degree costs $30,000 - $50,000. For that investment, we should expect elementary teachers to exit from their programs prepared to teach virtually all of their students to read on grade level without additional costly training by public schools."

–Paul Rosier, Superintendent, Kennewick School District

Learning to speak is a natural process. Children over the entire world learn to speak. Except for the deaf, in every country for thousands of years, children have learned to speak without formal instruction.

Learning to read is a less natural process. Over the last thousands of years, only a tiny portion of the human population has ever learned to read, and even today worldwide, there are perhaps a billion nonreaders.[1] Reading is a learned behavior, and teaching it uniformly to all children is a specialized art.

The first evidence of written language using a symbol for each word or concept appears in ancient Mesopotamia with the Sumerians.[2] This symbol system meant that only those with the time and financial means to memorize 5,000 symbols would be literate enough to have a reading vocabulary of 5,000 words. Egyptian hieroglyphics and the Chinese characters are better-known examples of this system.

---

[1] Vincent Greaney, "Reading in Developing Countries: Problems and Issues," in *Promoting Reading in Developing Countries,* edited by Vincent Greaney, (Washington, DC: International Reading Association/World Bank, 1996) 5-38.

[2] Marilyn Jager Adams, *Beginning to Read: Thinking and Learning about Print* (Cambridge, MA: MIT Press, 1990), 15-18.

These systems evolved into other writing systems that assigned symbols to sounds rather than to words/concepts.[5] It required only a handful of symbols, by comparison, to represent the comparatively few different sounds or syllables which made up the syllables or words in the language. English can trace its written ancestry straight back to the Phoenician alphabet. The greater efficiency of these writing systems (aided by the inevitable political fortunes of war) resulted in the general displacement of the one-symbol-per-word system by one-symbol-per-sound/syllable, except in the Far East. Many thousands more people could learn to read with much less effort.

> *"The definition of literacy changes to meet current needs; and the press for increased literacy today does not come from a decline in absolute levels, but from rising demands."[3]*
>
> *Four hundred years ago, literacy was defined as the ability to write one's name. Even by this standard, 42% of weavers, 50% of sailors, 75% of masons, 89% of women, and 90-97% of shepherds and thatchers were illiterate.[4]*

But there are significant differences between similar systems. Spanish has twenty-nine different alphabet symbols representing its thirty-one different oral sounds or phonemes. Because of its almost one-to-one correspondence between the alphabet symbols and oral sounds, it is an easy language to read. English uses nearly the same alphabet symbols but they represent forty-two to forty-four different sounds with only a general correspondence between the sounds and letters.[6] These difficulties materially complicate the task of teaching children to read.

Since the mid-1980s, a series of national commissions, reinforced by state and private initiatives, have documented the increasing demands for higher skills. Many states responded by calling for systemic school reform and greater accountability.

On the elementary level, whatever form the desired reform takes, the first challenge almost invariably is to significantly improve students' read-

---

[3] L. D. Stedman and C. E. Kaestle, "Literacy and Reading Performance in the United States from 1880 to the Present," *Reading Research Quarterly* 22 (1987): 8-46.

[4] David Cressy, "Levels of Illiteracy in England, 1530-1730," in *Literacy in Historical Perspective,* edited by Daniel P. Resnick (Washington, DC: Library of Congress, 1983), 108-9.

[5] For a short discussion of the areas of morphology (structure, form of words, inflection, derivation) and orthography (how language is represented by letters or other symbols), see Catherine E. Snow, M. Susan Burns, and Peg Griffin, eds., *Preventing Reading Difficulties in Young Children* (Washington, DC: National Research Council/National Academy Press, 1998), 21-23.

[6] Marathon Montrose Ramsey, *A Textbook of Modern Spanish,* rev. by Robert K. Spaulding (New York: Rinehart and Winston, 1967), 1.

ing ability. Most student-based school reform requires students to demonstrate their proficiency in reading, writing, math, and science in a system of tests. Students who do not read, or who read significantly below grade level, not only fail to master the curriculum but are unable to effectively take the state tests.

As this book has documented, reading demands and merits the lion's share of our educational team's attention in K-3. As this book also documents, parents can do much to make their children reading-ready, but primarily the school staff's job is to teach them how to read. In practical terms, it means that the enormous, complicated, and expensive structure of American education comes down to the quality and quantity of interactions between K-3 teachers and children.

> *"Our focus on chronological age blurs the huge differences in reading skill levels of incoming kindergarten and first graders. Our colleges do an adequate job of training K-3 teachers to take the highly skilled children to third grade reading level by third grade. Future K-3 teachers are not academically prepared to address the cognitive, visual, learning, and specific learning disabilities of the four to six lower-skilled children they will get in each classroom to third-grade reading level by third grade. Hence, the task of bringing all children to reading level becomes even greater."*
>
> —Marlis Lindbloom, Assistant Superintendent of Curriculum and Instructional Services, Kennewick School District

It may not be too much to say that the vast and complex educational enterprise in our nation comes down to Miss Caroline Starr, first-year kindergarten teacher in Room 3, holding up a poster of an ice cream cone illustrating the long "i" sound and asking, "Tony, what sound does it say?" Mindy already knows. How long will it take Tony to make the connection? And what else does Miss Starr have in her repertoire of skills besides the poster of the ice cream cone?

This chapter asks what elementary schools need from universities and colleges in preparing prospective teachers. Without question, our answer based on our recent experience, would be: Give them a stronger foundation in the teaching of reading.

Beginning teachers, particularly those in the primary grades, must have a solid repertoire of methods for teaching children to read. At present, most new teachers are not adequately prepared to teach about 40% of our challenging children to read.

Suggestions from the Field

These suggestions are based on on-going discussions in our district with practicing teachers and principals, supplemented by intensive conference sessions, seminars, and personal conversations with college instructors. They are field proposals, offered for further development, in the hope that a reality-grounded curriculum of study and training can be organized.

> "The gap that exists between the level of knowledge and what we have implemented of that knowledge all across the board . . . is absolutely awful and sad."
>
> —Sally Shaywitz[7]

1. Know the research. Any classroom teacher knows that no single approach to teaching reading meets the needs of all children. Children learn differently. Therefore, a teacher must have deep foundations of techniques and strategies to be successful. Research on reading over the past forty years has produced literally thousands of reports, and some of the most exciting research currently being done deals with reading.

Unfortunately, most of the research gets ignored, according to our principals, unless it advances a particular side of the phonics/whole language conflict. (See Appendix F.) This conflict over theories and models has no clear winners, but it certainly has losers. The children.

> "Phonemic awareness skills assessed in kindergarten and first grade serve as potent predictors of difficulties learning to read. With a test that takes only 15 minutes to administer, we have learned how to measure phonemic awareness skills as early as the beginning of kindergarten, and over the past decade we have refined these tasks so that we can predict with approximately 92% accuracy who will have difficulties learning to read."
>
> —G. Reid Lyon[8]

Admittedly, not all research is of equal merit, and some of it reflects fads and fashions now outdated. Still, a solid, thorough survey of the literature makes it clear that some practices are more effective than others. Teachers need to have a sound background in this research. It will provide a rich menu of options and save them from investing valuable time in reinventing already rolling wheels.

---

[7] Sally Shaywitz, Pediatrician-research scientist, Center for Learning and Attention, Yale University, qtd. in "Reading by Nine," *Baltimore Sun*, 2-5 Nov. 1997, 22.

[8] G. Reid Lyon, Ph.D., Chief of the Child Development and Behavior Branch of the National Institute of Child Health and Human Development (NICHD), National Institutes of Health (NIH), *Statement before the Committee on Education and the Workforce, U.S. House of Representatives, Washington, D.C., Thursday, July 10, 1997,* 9.

New research has revealed that reading engages three centers in the brain. If a child's brain cannot process information efficiently in any one of these three, then that child will have difficulty learning to read. Well-trained teachers can help compensate for these physiological difficulties, creating alternatives that will help these students become good readers by the end of the primary grades.

The greatest opportunity for improving the reading performance of our students occurs in the earliest years, K-3. The 40% of students who will have a difficult time learning to read can be identified with a fifteen-minute test in the first few months of kindergarten. Strategies to meet their needs must be implemented in kindergarten and first grade, and then reinforced in second and third grades, not in fourth grade where most remedial programs kick in.

2. **Stress application.** Prospective teachers in elementary school, especially those headed for K-3, need extensive exposure to, observations of, and practice in teaching reading. Dr. G. Reid Lyon, Chief of the Child Development and Behavior Branch of the National Institute of Child Health and Human Development (NICHD), National Institutes of Health, testified before the U.S. House of Representatives' Committee on Education and the Workforce:

> *"The data indicate that the ability to learn to read is remarkably independent of ethnicity and parental education and children's IQ. Everything we can measure says it depends on what they learn, which means it depends on what we teach them."*
>
> —Marilyn Jager Adams, *Beginning to Read: Thinking and Learning about Print* (Cambridge, MA: MIT Press, 1990).

"Most teachers receive little formal instruction in reading development and disorders during either undergraduate and/or graduate studies, with the average teacher completing only two reading courses. Surveys of teachers taking these courses indicate consistently that very few of them have ever observed professors demonstrating instructional reading methods with children; teachers also report that their course work is largely unrelated to actual teaching practices, that the theories they learn are rarely linked to the actual instruction of children, and that the supervision of student teaching and practicum experiences is frequently lacking in consistency and depth."

Teaching reading is an application process. It is not a discussion of theory, nor does it occur in an abstract world. Much of the problem in preparing new teachers to teach reading effectively is that teaching at institutions of higher learning presents theories, models, hypotheses. It does not get Miss Starr, her ice cream cone, and Tony in the same room with an experienced mentor to coach and encourage.

3. **Reshape the curriculum to provide observation.** The application-based experience with children now needed for prospective teachers requires the elimination of some of the lecture-and-seatwork to get candidates into classrooms where they can observe teachers at work. Observing classroom teachers teaching reading provides a repertoire of examples to anchor the abstractness of college-level lectures on theory and pedagogy.

4. **Reward volunteer tutoring.** Even though it may not be possible for a college of education to require or sponsor reading tutorials for their students, they should encourage teacher candidates to volunteer as tutors for individual children throughout their training years and find ways of rewarding such participation. This experience will create more realism in the training process.

5. **Teach strategies and methods.** All elementary teacher candidates need an extensive, possibly year-long, course in strategies and methods that emphasizes:

   - Structuring a balanced approach from the many different pedagogical methods available.

   - The components of reading, including phonemic awareness, word recognition skills/phonics, structural analysis, comprehension, literature-based approaches, the use of pattern books, predictable readers, phonics-based texts, big books, etc.

   - Reports from field practitioners and videotapes of the actual strategies in classroom use.

6. **Teach strategies for applied reading.** These strategies would focus on content, comprehension, technical nonfiction, and other forms of applied reading—using reading skills for learning. It should include hands-on introductions to the various types of resource materials, reference books, CDs, and the Internet. Again, using field practitioners as resource people or instructors would enhance effectiveness.

7. **Integrate literacy strategies and methods.** At least one course should concentrate on strategies for writing, spelling, speaking, and listening. Emphasis on writers' workshops, Six Traits writing skills,[9] phonetic spelling, and language experience could all be components of this course.

8. **Require a practicum in reading instruction for K-3 candidates.** We would recommend that this practicum include twenty hours of observing reading instruction, tutoring individual students for a minimum of twenty hours, preparing a comparative study of two initial reading approaches, preparing a reading unit for students, etc.

9. **Maximize student teaching.** The student teaching experience is the single most important component of teacher training. The best possible teachers—those with a positive record of teaching reading—should supervise classroom student teachers. The experience should be full time for a minimum of two semesters.

10. **Make mastery the goal.** The teacher training program should emphasize that all elementary teachers must master at least one approach to reading within the first two years of teaching. This approach should be the one used by the school where they are working. Few new teachers are ready to establish their own reading program. Only after a sound foundation in one reading approach is mastered should new teachers explore other approaches and strategies. The possibility of being overwhelmed, patching together a piecemeal approach that omits important skills, and not giving themselves enough time to become generally comfortable in the classroom are some of the problems.

11. **Require a reading endorsement or minor for all K-3 teachers..** Reading is the key to success in school, and it is the process skill to future learning. Nothing is more important in the curriculum. The better prepared these teachers are to teach reading, the better the chances for teaching all children to read well by the end of their primary grades.

12. **Institute accountability for the certification process itself.** Teacher college programs themselves need an accountability component. Just as seat time programs for students are proving inadequate, seat time certification programs for teachers are lacking. Second year teachers and their building principals should formally evaluate the effectiveness of their university program. Those evaluations should be available on the internet for each state.

---

[9] The Six Traits Writing Process was developed by the Northwest Regional Education Laboratory in Portland, Oregon. The six traits are sound ideas, good organization, voice, powerful words, fluency, and correct conventions.

In August 1998, the Education Trust, an organization dedicated to improving teaching for poor students, released a report based on studies in four states. This report highlights and underscores the power of well-trained and effective teachers. It rated teachers according to their education, experience, and test scores on licensing exams, then matched them with their students' performance. In Tennessee, children in the classrooms of the "least effective" teachers progressed about 14 percentile points during the year; the most effective teachers brought their low-achieving students up an average of 53 percentile points. In Texas, teacher quality explained "43 percent of the variance in student achievement." In Massachusetts, the top third of the teachers are producing "six times the learning" as the bottom third. In contrast to the current view that turn-around change comes from a charismatic and controversial principal, Education Trust director Kay Haycock asks a penetrating question: "What if these schools are succeeding not on the force of someone's personality but simply by teaching students what they need to know to perform at high levels?"[10]

A refocused curriculum and training program for elementary school teachers is much easier to suggest than to do. But our experience brings us back again and again to this bottom line: teacher preparation institutions need to make reading instruction the primary focus of prospective elementary teachers. Universities and colleges have the obligation of supplying the K-12 school system with teachers who have a good foundation in the most essential skill that they will teach—reading.

---

[10] E. J. Dionne, Jr., "Good Teachers Do Make a Difference," *Washington Post*, Aug. 11, 1998, A-21.

CHAPTER SIXTEEN

WHAT LEGISLATORS CAN DO

"If one in four tuna cans were contaminated, we would immediately shut down the industry. If one in four NASA rockets self-destructed, we would halt funding. If one in four children fail to learn to read early and well, then it will be only a matter of time before the legislature sets system performance standards as conditions of future funding."

—Senator Patricia Hale, Washington State Legislature

As board members, legislators, publishers and parents, we don't care who wins the phonetics/whole language war. We don't care because it is the wrong war. Substantial numbers of our children will not learn to read no matter which side wins. The right war is focusing on results.

Louisiana's instruction is primarily phonetics based, and Louisiana scored last among the states on the 1994 National Assessment of Educational Performance (NAEP) fourth-grade reading test. California's instruction was primarily whole language-based, and California's fourth graders scored second to last among the states of the 1994 NAEP fourth grade reading test.[1]

---

[1] Educational Testing Service (under contract with the National Center for Education Statistics), *NAEP 1994 Reading Report Card for the Nation and the States: Findings from the National Assessment of Educational Progress and Trial State Assessments* (Washington, DC: U.S. Department of Education Office of Educational Research and Improvement, Jan. 1996), 60. Actually, Guam was last; and the District of Columbia, which had been lower than California and Louisiana in 1992, dropped out.

There's a message here. No curriculum approach will teach reading automatically. Any curriculum can be used in ways that children don't learn. It is time to stop funding the intellectual wars of our educators. No politician or parent cares about the pedigree of a reading program that does not work for their child.

The Structure of Education: Seven Players

Every state has highly similar organizational structures growing out of the similar political requirements and funding formulas. Each state is divided geographically into educational districts. Each district is operated like a corporation. Each has a CEO/superintendent, with policy controlled by a board elected by the stakeholders.

The industry also has state-wide organizations:

- *for teachers*
- *for principals and superintendents*
- *for its publicly elected school board members.*

It also has:
- *A state-wide Parent-Teacher Association*
- *A state-level board (for example, New York has a Board of Regents)*
- *A state department of education*
- *Legislative education committees, one in both the House and the Senate (or their equivalent).*

Each of these associations has annual conventions. Each maintains lobbyists and positions on virtually every educational issue. Power ebbs and flows among these seven players. Each year, the first six groups come before the seventh to discuss the two things on which the first six all agree: (1) Education needs more money. (2) And the increase in money should not be conditioned on improved academic results.

We can end the war. The way we end the war is to simply say, We don't care about your methodology. We care about your results. We who are responsible for making public education work expect 90% of our third graders to read at or above grade level. We want demonstrable evidence every year from every classroom and from every school that substantially all of our third graders can read at grade level.

Any program that is not teaching 90% of its students to read fourth-grade textbooks written at a fourth-grade level by fourth grade needs improvement. And just because a program works across town, or just because it worked last year with last year's students isn't good enough any longer. It must work this year, with this year's students, in this school. Parachutists may debate styles of chutes and different ways to pack them, but there is one thing they do not debate. No matter what the brand name or how it is packaged, their parachute, when they jump, had better open. Parachutists, like our students, take no comfort in something that worked at a different time and place with a different person, but doesn't work for them.

Legislators must focus on results. Reading programs must work for their students, in their buildings. Teacher colleges, reading conferences, and State Departments of Education should continually emphasize results.

Legislators can stop the reading wars. They can do it by creating the goal, the tests, and the reporting systems to measure results. They must also leave the professionals in the elementary building and classroom free on how to achieve those results while holding them accountable for the achievement. It's the American way. It is also the only way that will work.

Every state can pass reading legislation which creates reading accountability at a state level. (See Appendix G for a model bill.) Legislation creating reading accountability should, at the minimum, achieve six results:

1. Set an achievable and measurable reading goal, or as an interim step, require each district to set its own.

2. Create and fund the measuring device—a basic reading test.

3. Set the reading standard on the test or create a process for setting the reading standard.

4. Report the results by the percentage of students at or above the standard, statewide, by district, by elementary building, and by student (to the parent or guardian). Count all the children in the denominator. Provide for the results to be reported that same school year.

5. Encourage parents to read aloud daily with their children.

6. Reward growth. When we reward success and not failure, we get more success and less failure.

CHAPTER SEVENTEEN

AND WHAT YOU CAN DO

"Do not doubt that a small band of determined citizens can change the world. Indeed, it is the only thing that ever has."

—Margaret Mead

"What can I do?" you are asking yourself. "It's true that this message speaks to me. It's true that this message rings with common sense. But who am I? Just a school board member, or just one of a hundred legislators, or a newspaper publisher dwarfed by the giant national dailies. The Rosiers, or the Kerrs, or the Fieldings may be able to do this in their district. Washington state, with its emerald Puget Sound and elegant Space Needle and suburban school systems—they can do this. But who am I?"

Who are we to try to solve this persistent problem? Who are we to eliminate illiteracy in America?

We are not U.S. senators. We are not college presidents or governors. We are mere school board members, mere superintendents, state legislators, and newspaper publishers. We are the ones who govern America's public schools, and we are the only ones who hold it accountable.

Perhaps this job could be done by business or higher education. Perhaps we could find a better place besides our public elementary schools to teach our children to read, and perhaps we can find someone besides parents to read to their children from birth.

But isn't this our job? "The future is in the hands," observed theologian-philosopher Teilhard de Chardin, "of those who can give tomorrow's generation a valid reason to hope." Isn't teaching children to read our first academic job as educators and as those responsible for educational governance?

Let's look again at the steps. The last chapter dealt with steps legislators can take. Which ones can we in the community take?

1. **Identify expectations and current performance.** The logical place to start is the place that will produce the most energy. That's the chasm between our public's reading expectations for children and our third grade reading reality. The power to change grows out of our willingness to be absolutely truthful about how many entering fourth graders read at a first-, second-, and third-grade level.

   We have positively marketed our schools. There will be a marked reluctance for administrations to provide their boards with this grim information. It may be much harder than we imagine to be candid with our parents, community, and newspaper publishers not only about the number of children reading below grade level, but at what grade level these children actually read as well.

   Ways of highlighting community expectations are simple.

   - Make an informal survey of board members, asking, "At what minimum level should third graders read?"

   - Hold a meeting with local newspaper publishers on expected elementary reading levels.

   - Conduct a school-by-school survey of parent expectations for reading levels in grades K-3.

   This exercise—if it is necessary—will quantify community expectations. What will be more necessary is quantifying current third- and fourth-grade reading levels.

   To quantify current reading levels, we must:

   - Convert current data from third and fourth grade nationally normed reading tests to grade-level equivalents for easy comprehensibility.

   - Calculate and report the percentage of students reading at or above grade level, using all enrolled students in the grade, school by school.

   These are all simple tasks for those who govern our schools—for legislators, board members, and superintendents. And the results are news for the newspaper publishers who represent the citizens in holding us accountable. These steps clarify the chasm between current public perception and current performance levels in reading. These steps tap into the energy that makes the next two steps inevitable.

2. **Choose good tests.** The next step is putting good tests in place. For as little as $3.50 per student, the Northwest Evaluation Association (NWEA) will score and provide reports for a third- or fourth-grade reading, math, or science test. The cost for providing the test varies according to district. (See Chapters 6 and 11.) Boards need to establish the policies requiring the testing and include in the budget the necessary funds. (See Chapters 5, 7, and 11.)

> "Until one is committed there is hesitancy, the chance to draw back, always ineffectiveness. Concerning all acts of initiative (and creation), there is one elementary truth, the ignorance of which kills countless ideas and splendid plans: that the moment one definitely commits oneself, then Providence moves, too. All sorts of things occur to help one that would never otherwise have occurred. The whole stream of events issues from the decision, raising in one's favor all manner of unforeseen incidents and meetings and material assistance, which no man could have dreamt would have come his way. I have learned a deep respect for one of Goethe's couplets: 'Whatever you can do, or dream you can, begin it. Boldness has genius, power and magic in it.'"
>
> —W. H. Murray, *The Scottish Himalayan Expedition*

In large districts the organizational structures should include a cabinet-level director of assessment. In smaller districts the function should be a major responsibility of the superintendent. The energy from the first step will make these actions fairly simple.

3. **Determine the goal,** put it in policy, and put the reporting format in place. (See Chapters 5 and 11.)

4. **Provide support.** At this juncture, the superintendent, board, and administrators need to think seriously about how to do things differently and how to provide district support for our professional educators who will find the ways to teach grade-level reading skills, one child at a time. (See Chapter 13.)

5. **Establish a Reading Foundation** in your community. Mobilize parent support. Make daily reading aloud something that every child experiences. (See Chapters 8, 9, and 14.)

So this is what you can do. Five steps. These are the five steps outlined in Chapter 5. They can be done in any district by any superintendent and board. We will help. This is our invitation.

APPENDIX A

Resource List

The National Institute for Child Health and Human Development is the single largest coordinator of research on early childhood literacy issues in the United State: http:www.NIH.gov/NICHD/publications.

Johns Hopkins University has extensive reading research including a website of Robert Slavin's writings at http:scov.csos.jhu.edu. Additional information is at Slavin's "Success for All" (see Chapter 5) and website: http:www.successforall.com

Willard Daggett is one of the foremost thinkers in K-12 educational reform and was a significant catalyst for change in Kennewick. International Center for Educational Leadership can be accessed at http:www.daggett.com.

Washington State's educational reform has focused on elementary reading accountability. With the full support of Governor Gary Locke, Superintendent of Public Education Terry Bergeson has focused the state on education's most basic skill. http:www.ospi.wednet.edu

Texas is another active state focusing on elementary reading. Its program is well thought out and has extraordinary support from its governor, George W. Bush. http:www.governor.state.tx.us

Toll-Free Texas Education Agency Reading Hotline 1-800-819-5713

Kennewick School District	http:www.ksd.org
Reading Foundation	http:www.reading foundation.org
	509-735-9405
Northwest Evaluation Association	http:www.nwea.org
Jim Trelease	
Reading Tree Productions	http:www.trelease-on-reading.com
America Reads Challenge	http:www.ed.gov.inits/americareads
Paul Rosier	http.www.rosipa@ksd.org
Nancy Kerr	http.www.kerrna@ksd.org
Lynn Fielding	http.www.lynnfielding@hotmail.com

APPENDIX B

Statement before the Committee of Labor and Human Resources, United States Senate, Washington, D.C., Tuesday, April 28, 1998.

G. Reid Lyon, Ph.D.
Chief of Child Development and Behavior Branch,
National Institute of Child Health and Human Development,
National Institutes of Health

Mr. Chairman and members of the committee:

I am Dr. Reid Lyon, the Chief of the Child Development and Behavior Branch of the National Institute of Child Health and Human Development at the National Institutes of Health. I am pleased to have this opportunity to present to you information about the results of the extensive research that our institute has supported on the process of learning to read in our nation's schools.

Some children learn to read and write with ease. Even before they enter school, they have developed an understanding that the letters on a page can be sounded out to make words, and some preschool children can even read words correctly that they have never seen before and comprehend what they have read. As Marilyn Adams has reported, before school, and without any great effort or pressure on the part of their parents, they pick up books, pencils, and paper, and they are on their way, almost as though by magic.

However, the magic of this effortless journey into the world of reading is available to only about 5% of our nation's children. It is suggested in the research literature that another 20% to 30% learn to read relatively easily once exposed to formal instruction, and it seems that youngsters in this group learn to read in any classroom, with any instructional emphasis.

Unfortunately, it appears that, for about 60% of our nation's children, learning to read is a much more formidable challenge; and for at least 20% to 30% of these youngsters, reading is one of the most difficult tasks that they will have to master throughout their schooling. Why is this so unfortunate? Simply because if you do not learn to read and you live in America, you do not make it in life. Consider that reading skill serves as the major avenue to learning about other people, about history and social studies, the language arts, science, mathematics, and the other content subjects that must be mastered in school. When children do not learn to read, their general knowledge, their spelling and writing abilities, and their vocabulary development suffer in kind. Within this context, reading skill serves as the major foundational skill for all school-based

---

Used by permission. Punctuation and capitalization edited to conform to the style used in this book. G. Reid Lyon made a similar, though not identical statement, which has been quoted at various points in this text, before the Committee on Education and the Workforce, U.S. House of Representatives, Washington, D.C., Thursday, July 10, 1997.

learning; and without it, the chances for academic and occupational success are limited indeed.

Because of its importance and visibility, particularly during the primary grades, difficulty in learning to read squashes the excitement and love for learning that many youngsters enter school with. It is embarrassing and even devastating to read slowly and laboriously and to demonstrate this weakness in front of peers on a daily basis. It is clear from our NICHD-supported longitudinal studies that follow good and poor readers from kindergarten into young adulthood that our young poor readers are quickly affected by their failure. By the end of the first grade, we begin to notice substantial decreases in the children's self-esteem, self-concept, and motivation to learn to read if they have not been able to master reading skills and keep up with their age-mates. As we follow the children through elementary and middle-school grades, these problems compound; and in many cases, very bright youngsters are unable to learn about the wonders of science, mathematics, literature, and the like because they cannot read the grade-level textbooks. By high school, these children's potential for entering college has decreased to almost nil, with few choices available to them with respect to occupational and vocational opportunities. These individuals constantly tell us that they hate to read, primarily because it is such hard work, and their reading is so slow and laborious. As one adolescent in one of our longitudinal studies remarked recently, "I would rather have a root canal than read."

While failure to learn to read adequately is much more likely among poor children, among nonwhite children, and among nonnative speakers of English, recent data derived from the National Assessment of Educational Progress (1994) reveals an alarming trend. In the State of California, 59% of fourth-grade children had little or no mastery of the knowledge and skills necessary to perform reading activities at the fourth-grade level, compared to a national average of 44% who are below basic reading levels.

Even more alarming is that this evidence of serious reading failure cuts across all ethnic and socioeconomic variables. While 71% of African-Americans, 81% of Hispanics, and 23% of Asians were reading below basic levels, 44% of white students in the fourth grade were also below the basic reading level necessary to use reading as a skill. Moreover, 49% of the fourth-grade children in California who were reading below basic levels were from homes where the parents had graduated from college. In fact, the children of college-educated parents in California scored lowest with respect to their national cohort. These data underscore the fact that reading failure is a serious national problem and cannot simply be attributed to poverty, immigration, or the learning of English as a second language. The psychological, social, and economic consequences of reading failure are legion.

It is for this reason that the National Institutes of Health considers reading failure to reflect not only an educational problem but a significant public health problem as well. Several NIH Institutes, including the National Institute of Neurological Disorders and Stroke, the National Institute of Mental Health, the National Institute of Deafness and Other Communication Disorders, and my institute, the National Institute of Child Health and Human Development (NICHD), support research to investigate the processes that relate to how children learn to read.

As the lead institute in this effort, the NICHD supports a large research network consisting of 41 research sites in North America, Europe, and Asia working hard to identify: (1) the critical environmental, experiential, cognitive, genetic, neurobiological, and instructional conditions that foster strong reading development; (2) the risk factors that predispose youngsters to reading failure; and (3) the instructional procedures that can be applied to ameliorate reading deficits at the earliest possible time. The NICHD has supported research to understand normal reading development and reading difficulties continuously since 1965. During the past 33 years, NICHD-supported scientists have studied the reading development of 34,501 children and adults. Many studies have been devoted to understanding the normal reading process, and 21,860 good readers have participated in investigations, some for as long as 12 years. Significant effort has also been deployed to understand why many children do not learn to read. To address this critical question, 12,641 individuals with reading difficulties have been studied, many for as long as 12 years. In addition, since 1985, the NICHD has initiated studies designed to develop early identification methods that can pinpoint children during kindergarten and the first grade who are at risk for reading failure. These studies have provided the foundation for several prevention and early intervention projects now underway at 11 sites in the United States and Canada. Since 1985, 7,669 children (including 1,423 good readers) have participated in these reading instruction studies, and 3,600 youngsters are currently enrolled in longitudinal early intervention studies in Texas, Washington, Georgia, Massachusetts, New York, Florida, Colorado, North Carolina, and Washington, D.C. These studies have involved the participation of 1,102 classroom teachers, working in 266 schools and 985 classrooms[1]

With this as background, my remaining testimony will focus on addressing several major questions that may be of interest to the Committee on Labor and Human Resources on the topic of this hearing, "Reading and Literacy Initiatives." These questions are:

1. How do children learn to read?

2. Why do some children (and adults) have difficulties learning to read?

3. How can we help children learn to read? That is, for which children are which teaching approaches most beneficial at which states of reading development?

How Do Children Learn to Read?

Understanding How Sounds Are Connected to Print

In general, learning to read the English language is not as easy as conventional wisdom would suggest. Every type of writing system, whether it be a syllabic system as used by the Japanese, a morphosyllabic system as used by the Chinese (where a written symbol represents a unit of meaning), or an alphabetic system that is used in English, Spanish, and Scandinavian languages (to name a few) present challenges to the beginning reader. For example, in an English alphabetic system, the individual letters on the page are abstract and meaningless, in and of themselves. They must eventually be linked to equally abstract sounds, called phonemes, blended together, and pronounced as words, where meaning is finally realized. To learn to read English, the child must figure out the relationship between sounds and letters. Thus, the beginning reader must learn the connections between the 40 or so sounds of spoken English (the phonemes), and the 26 letters of the alphabet. What our NICHD research has taught us is

---

[1] The original testimony included a summary of the NICHD Reading Research Program.

that in order for a beginning reader to learn how to connect or translate printed symbols (letters and letter patterns) into sound, the would-be reader must understand that our speech can be segmented or broken into small sounds (phoneme awareness) and that the segmented units of speech can be represented by printed forms (phonics). This understanding that written spellings systematically represent the phonemes of spoken words (termed the alphabetic principle) is absolutely necessary for the development of accurate and rapid word reading skills.

Why is phoneme awareness so critical for the beginning reader? Because if children cannot perceive the sounds in spoken words—for example, if they cannot "hear" the "at" sound in "fat" and "cat" and perceive that the difference lies in the first sound—they will have difficulty decoding or "sounding out" words in a rapid and accurate fashion. This awareness of the sound structure of our language seems so easy and commonplace that we take it for granted. But many children do not develop phoneme awareness—and for some interesting reasons that we are now beginning to understand. Unlike writing, the speech we use to communicate orally does not consist of separate sounds in words. For example, while a written word like "cat" has three letter-sound units, the ear hears only one sound, not three, when the word "cat" is spoken aloud. This merging and overlapping of sounds into a sound "bundle" makes oral communication much more efficient. Consider how long it would take to have a conversation if each of the words that we uttered were segmented or "chopped" into their sound structure. In essence we would be spelling aloud the words we were speaking.

From the NICHD studies that were initiated in 1965 to understand how the reading process develops, we now have strong evidence that it is not the ear that understands that a spoken word like "cat" is divided into three sounds and that these discrete sounds can be linked to the letters C-A-T; it is the brain that performs this function. In some youngsters, the brain seems to have an easy time processing this type of information. However, in many children the skill is learned only with difficulty and thus must be taught directly, explicitly, and by a well-trained and informed teacher. It has also become clear to us that the development of these critical early reading-related skills such as phoneme awareness and phonics are fostered when children are read to at home during the preschool years, when they learn their letter and number names, and when they are introduced at very early ages to concepts of print and literacy activities.

Does this mean that children who have difficulty understanding that spoken words are composed of discrete individual sounds that can be linked to letters suffer from brain dysfunction or damage? Not at all. It simply means that the neural systems that perceive the phonemes in our language are less efficient than in other children. This difference in neural efficiency can also be hypothesized to underlie the individual differences that we see every day in learning any skill such as singing, playing an instrument, constructing a house, painting a portrait, and the like. In some cases, our NICHD studies have taught us that the phonological differences we see in good and poor readers have a genetic basis. In other children, the differences seem to be attributable to a lack of exposure to language patterns and literacy-based interactions and materials during the preschool years.

As pointed out, the development of phoneme awareness, the development of an understanding of the alphabetic principle and the translation of these skills to the application of phonics in reading words are non-negotiable beginning reading skills that all children must master in order to understand what they read and to learn from their reading sessions. Printed letters and words are the basic data on which reading depends, and the emerging reader must be able to recognize accurately and quickly spelling patterns and their mappings to speech. To recapitulate, these skills are supported nicely when children receive an abundance of early literacy experiences in the home and in preschool. But the development of phoneme awareness and phonics, while necessary, are not sufficient for learning to read the English language so that meaning can be derived from print. In addition to learning how to "sound out" new or unfamiliar words, the beginning reader must eventually become proficient in reading, at a very fast pace, larger units of print such as syllable patterns, meaningful roots, suffixes, and whole words.

The Development of Reading Fluency

While the ability to read words accurately is a necessary skill in learning to read, the speed at which this is done becomes a critical factor in ensuring that children understand what they read. As one child recently remarked, "If you don't ride a bike fast enough, you fall off." Likewise, if the reader does not recognize words quickly enough, the meaning will be lost. Although the initial stages of reading for many students require the learning of phoneme awareness and phonics principles, substantial practice of those skills, and continual application of those skills in text, fluency, and automaticity in decoding and word recognition must be acquired as well. Consider that a young reader (and even older readers for that matter) has only so much attentional capacity and cognitive energy to devote to a particular task. If the reading of the words on the page is slow and labored, readers simply cannot remember what they have read, much less relate the ideas they have read about to their own background knowledge. Children vary in the amount of practice that is required for fluency and automaticity in reading to occur. Some youngsters can read a word only once to recognize it again with greater speed; others need twenty or more exposures. The average child needs between four and fourteen exposures to automatize the recognition of a new word. Therefore, in learning to read, it is vital that children read a large amount of text at their independent reading level (95% accuracy), and that the text format provides specific practice in the skills being learned.

Constructing Meaning from Print

The ultimate goal of reading instruction is to enable children to understand what they read. Again, the development of phoneme awareness, phonics skills, and the ability to read words fluently and automatically are necessary but not sufficient for the construction of meaning from text. The ability to understand what is read appears to be based on several factors. Children who comprehend well seem to be able to activate their relevant background knowledge when reading—that is, they can relate what is on the page to what they already know. Good comprehenders also have good vocabularies, since it is extremely difficult to understand something you cannot define. Good comprehenders also have a knack for summarizing, predicting, and clarifying what they have read, and frequently use questions to guide their understanding. Good comprehenders are also facile in employing the sentence structure within the text to enhance their comprehension.

In general, if children can read the words on a page accurately and fluently, they will be able to construct meaning at two levels. At the first level, literal understanding is achieved. However, constructing meaning requires far more that literal comprehension. Children must eventually guide themselves through text by asking questions like "Why am I reading this and how does this information relate to my reasons for doing so?, What is the author's point of view?, Do I understand what the author is saying and why?, Is the text internally consistent?," and so on. It is this second level of comprehension that leads readers to reflective, purposeful understanding.

The development of reading comprehension skills, like the development of phoneme awareness, phonics, and fluency, needs to be fostered by highly trained teachers. Recent research shows that the teacher must arrange for opportunities for students to discuss the highlights of what they have read and any difficulties they have had when reading. Because the grammatical structures of written text are more varied and complex than those of casual, oral language (speaking to one another), regular exploration of and explicit instruction on formal syntax is warranted. Children's reflections on what they have read can also be directly fostered through instruction in comprehension strategies. These sorts of discussions and activities should be conducted throughout a range of literacy genres, both fiction and nonfiction, and should be a regular component of the language arts curriculum throughout the children's school years.

Other Factors That Influence Learning to Read

Our research continues to converge on the following findings. Good readers are phonemically aware and understand the alphabetic principle and can apply these skills to the development and application of phonics skills when reading stories, and can accomplish these applications in a fluent and accurate manner. Given the ability to rapidly and automatically decode and recognize words, good readers bring strong vocabularies and good syntactic and grammatical skills to the reading comprehension process, and actively relate what is being read to their own background knowledge via a variety of strategies. But what factors can provide a firm foundation for these skills to develop?

It is clear from research on emerging literacy that learning to read is a relatively lengthy process that begins very early in development and clearly before children enter formal schooling. Children who receive stimulating literacy experiences from birth onward appear to have an edge when it comes to vocabulary development, an understanding of the goals of reading, and an awareness of print and literacy concepts. Children who are read to frequently at very young ages become exposed in interesting and exciting ways to the sounds of our language, to the concept of rhyming, and to other word and language play that serves to provide the foundation for the development of phoneme awareness. As children are exposed to literacy activities at young ages, they begin to recognize and discriminate letters. Without a doubt, children who have learned to recognize and print most letters as preschoolers will have less to learn upon school entry. The learning of letter names is also important because the names of many letters contain the sounds they most often represent, thus orienting youngsters early to the alphabetic principle or how letters and sounds connect. Ultimately, children's ability to understand what they are reading is inextricably linked to their background knowledge. Very young children who are provided opportunities to learn, think, and talk about new areas of knowledge will gain much from the reading process. With understanding comes the clear desire to read more and to read frequently, ensuring that reading practice takes place.

Why Do Some Children (and Adults) Have Difficulties Learning to Read?

Difficulties learning to read result from a combination of factors. In general, children who are most at risk for reading failure are those who enter school with limited exposure to language and who have little prior understanding of concepts related to phonemic sensitivity, letter knowledge, print awareness, the purposes of reading, and general verbal skills, including vocabulary. Children raised in poverty, youngsters with limited proficiency in English, children with speech and hearing impairments, and children from homes where the parents' reading levels are low are relatively predisposed to reading failure. Likewise, youngsters with subaverage intellectual capabilities have difficulties learning to read, particularly in the reading comprehension domain.

Given this general background, recent research has been able to identify and replicate findings which point to at least four factors that hinder reading development among children irrespective of their socioeconomic level and ethnicity. These four factors include deficits in phoneme awareness and the development of the alphabetic principle (and the accurate and fluent application of these skills to textual reading), deficits in acquiring reading comprehension strategies and applying them to the reading of text, the development and maintenance of motivation to learn to read, and the inadequate preparation of teachers.

Deficits in Phoneme Awareness and the Development of the Alphabetic Principle

In essence, children who have difficulties learning to read can be readily observed. The signs of such difficulty are a labored approach to decoding or "sounding" unknown or unfamiliar words and repeated misidentification of known words. Reading is hesitant and characterized by frequent starts and stops and multiple mispronunciations. If asked about the meaning of what has been read, the child frequently has little to say—not because he or she is not smart enough; in fact, many youngsters who have difficulty learning to read are bright and motivated to learn to read—at least initially. Their poor comprehension occurs because they take far too long to read the words, leaving little energy for remembering and understanding what they have read.

Unfortunately, there is no way to bypass this decoding and word recognition stage of reading. A deficiency in these skills cannot be appreciably offset by using context to figure out the pronunciation of unknown words. In essence, while one learns to read for the fundamental purpose of deriving meaning from print, the key to comprehension starts with the immediate and accurate reading of words. In fact, difficulties in decoding and word recognition are at the core of most reading difficulties. To be sure, there are some children who can read words accurately and quickly yet do have difficulties comprehending, but they constitute a small portion of those with reading problems.

If the ability to gain meaning from print is dependent upon fast, accurate, and automatic decoding and word recognition, what factors hinder the acquisition of these basic reading skills? As mentioned above, young children who have a limited exposure to both oral language and print before they enter school are at risk for reading failure. However, many children with robust oral language experience, average to above intelligence, and frequent interactions with books since infancy show surprising difficulties learning to read. Why?

In contrast to good readers who understand that segmented units of speech can be linked to letters and letter patterns, poor readers have substantial difficulty developing this "alphabetic principle." The culprit appears to be a deficit in phoneme awareness—the understanding that words are made up of sound segments called phonemes. Difficulties in developing phoneme awareness can have genetic and neurobiological origins or can be attributable to a lack of exposure to language patterns and usage during the preschool years. The end result is the same however. Children who lack phoneme awareness have difficulties linking speech sounds to letters—their decoding skills are labored and weak, resulting in extremely slow reading. This labored access to print renders comprehension impossible. Thus the purpose for reading is nullified because the children are too dysfluent to make sense out of what they read.

In studying approximately 34,501 children over the past 33 years, we have learned the following with respect to the role that phonemic awareness plays in the development of phonics skills and fluent and automatic word reading:

1. Phonemic awareness skills assessed in kindergarten and first grade serve as potent predictors of difficulties in learning to read. We have learned how to measure phonemic awareness skills as early as the first semester in kindergarten. Over the past decade we have refined these tasks so that, with a test that takes only 15 minutes to administer, we can predict with approximately 80% to 90% accuracy who will become good readers and who will have difficulties in learning to read.

2. We have learned that the development of phonemic awareness is a necessary but not sufficient condition for learning to read. A child must integrate phonemic skills into the learning of phonics principles, must practice reading so that word recognition becomes rapid and accurate, and must learn how to actively use comprehension strategies to enhance meaning.

3. We have begun to understand how genetics are involved in learning to read, and this knowledge may ultimately contribute to our prevention efforts through the assessment of family reading histories.

4. We are entering very exciting frontiers in understanding how early brain development can provide a window on how reading develops. Likewise, we are conducting studies to help us understand how specific teaching methods change reading behavior and how the brain changes as reading develops.

5. We have learned that just as many girls as boys have difficulties learning to read. Until five years ago, the conventional wisdom was that many more boys than girls had such difficulties. Now females should have equal access to screening and intervention programs.

6. We have learned that for 90% to 95% of poor readers, prevention and early intervention programs that combine instruction in phoneme awareness, phonics, fluency development, and reading comprehension strategies, provided by well-trained teachers, can increase reading skills to average reading levels. However, we have also learned that if we delay intervention until nine years of age (the time that most children with reading difficulties receive services), approximately 75% of the children will continue to have difficulties learning to read throughout high school. To be clear, while older children and adults can be taught to read, the time and expense of doing so is enormous.

Deficits in Acquiring Reading Comprehension Strategies

Some children encounter obstacles in learning to read because they do not derive meaning from the material that they read. In the later grades, higher order comprehension skills become paramount for learning. Reading comprehension places significant demands on language comprehension and general verbal abilities. Constraints in these areas will typically limit comprehension. In a more specific vein, deficits in reading comprehension are related to: (1) inadequate understanding of the words used in the text; (2) inadequate background knowledge about the domains represented in the text; (3) a lack of familiarity with the semantic and syntactic structures that can help to predict the relationships between words; (4) a lack of knowledge about different writing conventions that are used to achieve different purposes via text (humor, explanation, dialogue, etc.); (5) verbal reasoning ability which enables the reader to "read between the lines"; and (6) the ability to remember verbal information.

If children are not provided early and consistent experiences that are explicitly designed to foster vocabulary development, background knowledge, the ability to detect and comprehend relationships among verbal concepts, and the ability to actively employ strategies to ensure the understanding and retention of material, reading failure will occur no matter how robust word recognition skills are.

Our current understanding of how to develop many of these critical language and reasoning capabilities related to reading comprehension is not as well developed as the information related to phoneme awareness, phonics, and reading fluency. We have not yet obtained clear answers with respect to why some children have a difficult time learning vocabulary and how to improve vocabulary skills. Our knowledge about the causes and consequences of deficits in syntactical development is sparse. A good deal of excellent research has been conducted on the application of reading comprehension strategies, but our knowledge of how to teach children to apply these strategies in an independent manner and across contexts is just emerging.

The Development and Maintenance of Motivation to Learn to Read

A major factor that aids or limits the amount of improvement that children may make in reading is highly related to their motivation to persist in learning to read despite difficulties. Very little is known with respect to the exact timing and course of motivational problems in reading development, but it is clear that reading failure has a devastating effect on children. In the primary grades, reading activities constitute the major portion of academic activities undertaken in classrooms, and children who struggle with reading are quickly noticed by peers and teachers.

Although most children enter formal schooling with positive attitudes and expectations for success, those who encounter difficulties in learning to read clearly attempt to avoid engaging in reading behavior as early as the middle of the first-grade year. It is known that successful reading development is predicated on practice in reading, and obviously the less a child practices, the less developed the various reading skills will become. To counter these highly predictable declines in the motivation to learn to read, prevention and early intervention programs are critical.

Preparation of Teachers

As evidence mounts that reading difficulties originate in large part from difficulties in developing phoneme awareness, phonics, reading fluency, and reading comprehension strategies, the need for informed instruction for the millions of children with insufficient reading skills is an increasingly urgent problem. Unfortunately, several recent studies and surveys of teachers' knowledge about reading development and difficulties indicate that many teachers are underprepared to teach reading. Most teachers receive little formal instruction in reading development and disorders during either undergraduate and / or graduate studies, with the average teacher completing only two reading courses. Surveys of teachers taking these courses indicate: (1) teachers rarely have the opportunity to observe professors demonstrate instructional reading methods with children; (2) coursework is frequently superficial and typically unrelated to teaching practice; and (3) the supervision of student teaching and practicum experiences is fragmentary and inconsistent. At present, motivated teachers are often left to obtain specific skills in teaching phonemic awareness, phonics, reading fluency, and comprehension on their own by seeking out workshops or specialized instructional manuals.

Teachers who instruct youngsters who display reading difficulties must be well versed in understanding the conditions that have to be present for children to develop robust reading skills. They also must be thoroughly trained to assess and identify children at risk for reading failure at early ages. Unfortunately, many teachers and administrators have been caught between conflicting schools of thought about how to teach reading and how to help students who are not progressing easily. In reading education, teachers are frequently presented with a "one size fits all" philosophy that emphasizes either a "whole language" or "phonics" orientation to instruction. No doubt, this parochial type of preparation places many children at continued risk for reading failure since it is well established that no grading program should be without all the major components of reading instruction (phoneme awareness, phonics, fluency, reading comprehension) and the real question is which children need what, how, for how long, with what type of teacher, and in what type of setting.

It is hard to find disagreement in the educational community that the direction and fabric of teacher education programs in language arts and reading must change. However, bringing about such change will be difficult. In addition, if teacher preparation in the area of language and reading is expected to become more thoughtful and systematic, changes in how teaching competencies and certification requirements are developed and implemented are a must. Currently, in many states, the certification offices within state departments of education do not maintain formal and collaborative relationships with academic departments within colleges of education. Thus, the requirements that a student may be expected to satisfy for a college degree may bear little relationship to the requirements for a teaching certificate. More alarming is the fact that both university and state department of education requirements for the teaching of reading may not reflect, in any way, the type and depth of knowledge that teachers must have to ensure literacy for all.

How Can We Help Children Learn to Read?

That is, for which children are which teaching approaches most beneficial at which stages of reading development?

1. Learning to read is a lengthy and difficult process for many children, and success in learning to read is based in large part on developing language and literacy-related skills very early in life. A massive effort needs to be undertaken to inform parents and the educational and medical communities of the need to involve children in reading from the first days of life—to engage children in playing with language through nursery rhymes, storybooks, and writing activities, to bring to children as early as possible experiences that help them understand the purposes of reading, and the wonder and joy that can be derived from reading. Parents must become intimately aware of the importance of vocabulary development and the use of verbal interaction with their youngsters to enhance grammar, syntax, and verbal reasoning.

2. Young preschool children should be encouraged to learn the letters of the alphabet, to discriminate letters from one another, to print letters, and to attempt to spell words that they hear. By introducing young children to print, their exposure to the purposes of reading and writing will increase and their knowledge of the conventions of print and their awareness of print concepts will increase.

3. Reading out loud to children is a proven activity for developing vocabulary growth and language expansion and plays a causal role in developing both receptive and expressive language capabilities. Reading out loud can also be used to enhance children's background knowledge of new concepts that may appear in both oral and written language.

4. Our NICHD prevention and early intervention studies in Houston, Tallahassee, Albany, Syracuse, Atlanta, Boston, Seattle, and Washington, D.C., all speak to the importance of early identification and intervention with children at risk for reading failure. Procedures now exist to identify such children with good accuracy. This information needs to be widely disseminated to schools, teachers, and parents.

5. Kindergarten programs should be designed so that all children will develop the prerequisite phonological, vocabulary, and early reading skills necessary for success in the first grade. All children should acquire the ability to recognize and print both upper- and lowercase letters with reasonable ease and accuracy, develop familiarity with the basic purposes and mechanisms of reading and writing, and develop age-appropriate language comprehension skills.

6. Beginning reading programs should be constructed to ensure that adequate instructional time is allotted to the teaching of phonemic awareness skills, phonics skills, the development of reading fluency and automaticity, and the development of reading comprehension strategies. All of these components of reading are necessary but not sufficient in and of themselvess. For children demonstrating difficulty in learning to read, it is imperative that each of these components be taught within an integrated context and that ample practice in reading familiar material be afforded. For some children, our research demonstrates that explicit, systematic instruction is crucial in helping them to understand and apply critical phonemic, phonics, fluency, and reading comprehension skills. Even for children who seem to grasp reading concepts easily, learning to read is not a natural process—reading instruction must be thoughtful and planned, and must incorporate the teaching of all the critical reading skills.

7. A major impediment to serving the needs of children demonstrating difficulties in learning to read is current teacher preparation practices. Many teachers lack basic knowledge about the structure of the English language, reading development, and the nature of reading difficulties. Major efforts should be undertaken to ensure that colleges of education possess the expertise and commitment to foster expertise in teachers at both preservice levels.

8. The preparation of teachers and the teaching of reading in our nation's classrooms must be based upon research evidence of the highest caliber and relevance. Research that is used to guide policy and instructional practice should be characterized by methodological rigor and the convergence of studies demonstrated to be representative, reliable, valid, and described with sufficient clarity and specificity to permit independent replication. Moreover, we must realize that no one study should be used to guide practice. To reiterate a significant point, the research knowledge that is employed to guide policy and practice must inform us how different components of reading behavior are best developed by various approaches to reading instruction for children of differing backgrounds, learning characteristics, and literacy experiences.

APPENDIX C

The Third Grade Reading Span in Raw Scores, Kennewick Elementary Schools, Fall 1995

This table is the basis for the percentage of incoming third graders reading at each level which appears in Chapter 3, Fig. 3.1. The full-range functional-level testing shows the eight-year reading range by the beginning of third grade. Southgate's third grades, for example, had five children reading at a kindergarten level, eight at a first-grade level, fourteen at a second grade level, and the rest at a third-grade level or above—including two at a seventh-grade level, and one at an eighth-grade level.

Grade Level		K	1	2	3	4	5	6	7	8	
Raw RIT	From:	140	175	185	192	199	206	212	217	221	No. of
Scores[1]	To:	174	184	191	198	205	211	216	220	226	Students
Amistad		17	11	10	11	5	7	7[2]	5[2]	3[2]	76
Canyonview		11	9	13	11	12	7	2	3	0	68
Cascade		10	17	11	21	28	4	4	-	-	95
Eastgate		15	8	14	16	4	3	-	-	-	60
Edison		10	9	11	12	10	3	2	-	-	57
Hawthorne		4	6	8	11	10	4	2	-	-	45
Lincoln		3	4	3	14	16	14	4	1	1	60
Ridge View		13	10	8	28	9	9	2	6	2	87
Southgate		5	8	14	16	16	6	5	2	1	73
Sunset View		4	15	11	19	16	16	8	1	2	92
Vista		3	10	15	11	11	6	3	0	-	59
Washington		15	12	15	12	6	4	1	-	-	65
Westgate		9	12	9	16	7	2	-	1	1	57
Total students		**119**	**131**	**142**	**198**	**150**	**85**	**40**	**19**	**10**	**894**
Percent of third graders at each grade level		13	14	16	22	17	10	5	2	1	

---

[1] The Northwest Evaluation Association provided the conversion from the RIT scores to grade level equivalents for grades 3 through 8. Kennewick School District provided the conversion to K-2 equivalents.

[2] The students reported as reading at the 6th, 7th and 8th grade level at this school are students in the district's gifted program.

Appendix D

Retention of Reading Progress As Measured by Percentage of Kennewick Fourth and Fifth Graders Meeting the District Reading Standard[1]

School	Fourth Grade[2] Spring 1998	Fifth Grade[2] Spring 1998
Amistad	59%	71%
Canyon View	80%	72%
Cascade	80%	79%
Eastgate	54%	66%
Edison	76%	80%
Hawthorne	77%	72%
Lincoln	77%	80%
Ridge View	84%	86%
Southgate	84%	84%
Sunset View	93%	92%
Vista	80%	81%
Washington	77%	76%
Westgate	53%	54%
District	**74%**	**77%**

[1] The reading standard at fourth grade is an NWEA RIT score of 199. The standard at fifth grade is an NWEA RIT score of 206.

[2] Percentages are figured on total number of students enrolled.

APPENDIX E   THE KENNEWICK STRATEGIC PLAN

GOAL #1. ENSURE THAT OUR SCHOOLS AND CLASSROOMS ARE SAFE AND ORDERLY.

SUBGOAL	PERSON[1]	DUE[2]	INDICATOR
1.1 Develop baseline report and improve the significant indicators of safety and order for our buildings, the district, and transportation.	Principals Transportation Greg Fancher Othene Bell Transportation	Sept 98 Sept 98 Sept 98 Fall 98	Specific indicators in building plan for goal. Specific indicators in annual plan for goal. Use 1997-98 baseline data to measure progress toward improvement at each school. Develop a community plan to increase school safety.
1.2 Identify those students with disruptive, violent, or toxic classroom behavior. Involve parents, civic, religious, and other community leaders as well as school personnel in altering the student behavior or place them in an alternative setting.	Paul Rosier Principals Greg Fancher Othene Bell M. Lindbloom	Ongoing Spring 98	Continue current community emphasis with FOCUS and other community groups. A report to the Board on resources needed to provide PSR training to all students in elementary and middle schools.
1.3 Continue the NO TOLERANCE POLICY towards weapons and violence.	Board Principals	Ongoing Oct 98	Reports: See 1.1 above. Obtain all parent's signatures on summaries of significant student policies sent home with Impact Aid Forms (Form 874).
1.4 Develop computer-video interact software on district policies regarding safety.	Paul Rosier	Fall 98 Spring 99	Seek out vendor to develop programs. Implement in selected schools.

Note: The Strategic Plan has been slightly edited for formatting purposes.

---

[1] Responsible party/parties include those supervising the listed individual/s.

[2] A short written achievement report on the indicator is due from the responsible person on the timeline date.

GOAL #2.   ACHIEVE THE 3RD GRADE READING GOAL: 90 % OF ALL THIRD GRADERS READING ON OR ABOVE GRADE LEVEL.

SUBGOAL	PERSON	DUE	INDICATOR
2.1 90% of third grade students will read at grade level or above by the end of the third grade.	Board	Monthly/ Bimonthly	Continue monthly school report meetings with the Board.
	Elementary Principals	June 99	Report of results of spring testing.
	Greg Fancher Bev Henderson	98-99	Establish a K-1 reading assessment system.
	Greg Fancher Bev Henderson	Fall 98 & Spring 99	Implement Functional Level Testing at 2nd grade.
	Principals	Fall 98-99	Develop a plan to address "mobile" students.
	Board	98-99	Levy funding commitment to elementary and secondary reading continued.
	Georgia Talbert Board	Fall 98	Internet access to building programs and reading assessment results.
2.2 Continue Support for The Reading Foundation.	Paul Rosier Nancy Kerr	98-99	Measurement of community awareness of the 20-minutes-daily reading expectations using voice poll process.
		98-99	Measurement of participation of 20-minutes-daily reading K-3 using voice poll and other strategies.
	H.S. Principals Nancy Kerr	Oct 97- June 98	Create internal partners with concurrence of The Reading Foundation that encourage older students to read 20 minutes a day with younger children.

GOAL #3. IMPLEMENT GRADE LEVEL STANDARDS/ ASSESSMENTS/ REPORTS AND ACCOUNTABILITY.

SUBGOAL	PERSON	DUE	INDICATOR
3.1 The District will develop and administer grade level assessments for core subjects at[3] the beginning and end of each school year, where appropriate. The assessment instructions will be coordinated with national and international learning standards and directly test the state Essential Academic Learning Standards.	Bev Henderson	Fall 98	Select and implement 2nd grade reading test.
	Bev Henderson	Spring 99	Administer district-wide Functional Level Tests in reading & math in grades 2-10.
	Bev Henderson	April 99	District-wide science testing.
	H.S. Science Chairs Principals Jim McLean	May 99	Concept paper on 9-10 grade science preparing for state 10th grade Certificate of Mastery test. Extension of Functional Level Testing through grade 10
	Georgia Talbert	May 99	Administer district-wide technology testing 3-8 to selected classes.
	M. Lindbloom Bev Henderson	April 98-2000	Implement state assessment instruments at grades 4, 7, & 10.
		98-99	Design and report an age appropriate verbal communications skills assessment 6-12 within the existing Language Arts program for post-secondary education, career/skill paths, and direct school-to-work-transition.
	M. Lindbloom	Ongoing	Instructional Council will verify the measurement of student learning in each new course prior to forwarding for Board approval.
	G. Wishkoski Jim McLean	98-99	Find a way to convert performance level scores to vertical-grade level measurements.

[3] The assessments will test curricula which prepare students for post secondary education and/or work. Course offering and course content K-12 shall be justified in terms of relevance to post-secondary education, work, transmission of culture, and personal development as well as coordinated with state, national, and international academic learning standards.

3.2 The District will develop a high school exit testing program to assess skill level and retention of subject content relevant to post high school education, training, and work.[4] Tests will be used to create differentiated diploma endorsements.	Othene Bell M. Lindbloom	Ongoing	Prepare and administer upon request, challenge tests for high school courses. The tests shall not exceed 3 hours in length, and be substantially similar to comprehensive course finals.
	M. Lindbloom	Jan/July 99	Establish articulation agreements for community college credit based on competency tests in language, math, sciences, history and relevant courses. (Board Report)
3.3 The District will develop grade level standards.	Paul Rosier Principals	Ongoing	Use grade level standards as components of District accountability process. Explore weighting IB and AP courses for determining valedictorian and salutatorian.
3.4 The District will develop and implement system and student accountability.[5]	M.S. Principals Othene Bell Jack Anderson Greg Fancher	Ongoing	Continue Middle School Accountability Plan. Continue developing programs for students of other levels, to post-HS ed. and to work. Implement elem. accountability standards.

[4] **Choice:** Students and parents will be provided options and will make academic decision based upon post-secondary objectives.

[5] **Mastery:** Our students will meet essential academic learning standards in language arts, mathematics, science, technology, social studies, the arts, world languages, health and wellness at a mastery level commensurate with the student's post-secondary future.

Accountability: A plan will be developed which will require students to demonstrate performance that meets established proficiency levels at selected points in their school careers. Students who fail to demonstrate proficiency may not advance or may receive alternative educational opportunities.

Alternate Learning Experiences: Develop and implement alternative and/or extended learning experiences for students not satisfying standards for the benchmark assessments. Individual student performance on functional level reading and math assessments will be expected to reflect one year's growth between fall and spring as measured by their Rasch Unit Scores (RIT) which will be used to establish grade level performance. The RIT Unit is the basic statistic used by the publisher of the functional level test to measure growth. Scores are expected to reflect one year's growth between fall and spring as measured by their Rasch Unit Scores (RIT) which will be used to establish grade level performance. Average student performance on norm-referenced exams (total Battery) at grades 4, 8, and 11 will reflect growth each year. The number of students with scores in the three highest quartiles will be expected to increase each year. Individual student performance on District performance assessments also will demonstrate continuous growth as measured by their Rubric Scores. Assessments will be identified or developed to measure performance on benchmarks at grades 5, 8, and 10 (or 11).

Goal	Responsible	Timeline	Activities
3.5 The District will create and produce stable reports of student academic achievement by student, school and District. The reports will include annual student growth, students meeting minimum, expected, and exceptional standards by building.	M. Lindbloom G. Clemans	Ongoing	Create and maintain a single integrated database of all significant assessments and indices of academic performances by students, building, and District groups of students.
	Bev Henderson G. Clemans Assess. Comm.	Spring 99	Provide grade-level equivalence on all functional level reports to parents.
	M. Lindbloom Linda Cameron Principals	June 98	An annual report will be prepared for public distribution outlining student assessment results including building reports and a District composite. The building reports will also outline improvement programs underway in each building.
3.6 To increase the percentage of students who enroll as 9th graders and actually graduate to 95% without compromising high standards.	Paul Rosier H. S. Principals	Fall 98 May 98-2000	Develop criteria for graduation rate. Develop a feasibility plan to establish a graduation rate goal with a 95% level.
3.7 Technical Skills for the Workplace: Determine current global standards for technical education and preparation. Plan for ways to incorporate technical skills such as those found in Principles of Technology and Materials Science into the mathematics, science, and technology curriculum so that students will graduate with strong technical skills.	M. Lindbloom Bob Eckert	99-2000	Develop concept paper with following: • Continue to refine integrated tech. lab. • Specific plans for the implementation of integrated tech. programs in grades 6-8.
	M. Lindbloom Georgia Talbert D. McClary		Identify and develop a plan to provide a core set of technological skills to be included in middle school and high school offerings that would be considered essential to a large number of skill pathways.
3.8 Systematically strengthen our core curriculum K-12.	M. Lindbloom	98-99	Refine the K-12 District Curriculum Frameworks in math, science, language arts, social studies, physical education, health, world language and the arts that are aligned to state essential academic learnings.
3.9 World Language	World Language Dept.	98-99	Baseline the number of 8th and 12th graders who have mastered a second language.

GOAL #4. ESTABLISH A DISTRICT-WIDE CUSTOMER FOCUS.

SUBGOAL	PERSON	DUE	INDICATOR
4.1 PRIMARY FOCUS			
4.1.1 Each school and major district department will develop and implement a customer focus improvement plan based on the results of the Black Customer Satisfaction Survey.	Principals Managers	Ongoing	Follow P-D-C-A Approach.
4.2 SECONDARY FOCUS			
4.2.1 Annually conduct a written survey of the stakeholders in each co-curricular and student support program including, attitude and participation.	Othene Bell	Ongoing	Administer instrument at middle school level. Collate data and report. Administer instrument at high school level at the completion of each sports season. Review and revise instruments. Collate data and report.
4.2.2 An Individual Student Growth Plan (ISGP) is developed or reviewed annually with the student, teacher, and parent or guardian. In the elementary grades, the ISGP will identify and nurture single topics of intense interest and passion to the student. By high school, the ISGP identifies potential career paths, corresponding courses of study, and the amount and sources of funding for post-secondary education.	Greg Fancher Othene Bell	Ongoing	Continue to implement the ISGP at all levels.
4.2.3 Teach and test the costs and savings necessary to fund post-secondary education and the earning power differentials resulting from additional post-secondary education and training starting in the 5th grade.	M. Lindbloom Bev Henderson Principals	Mar 99	Develop a test segment for 5th, 6th, 7th, 8th,+9th grade. Include in district-wide testing.

Action	Responsibility	Timeline	Notes
		Ongoing	At the middle school and high school levels introduce the concepts of skill paths and their implications for lifelong learning including the need for and cost of post high school education.
		Ongoing	Implement poster campaign of facts about careers, lifelong earnings, cost of post-high school education.
4.2.4 Encourage the involvement of every 6-12 grade student in at least one co-curricular program or activity beyond the classroom which provides opportunity for students to experience success.	Othene Bell		On Hold
4.2.5 Focus on living a healthy lifestyle increasing in the emphasis on lifelong activities, including student avoidance of alcohol, tobacco, and other drugs.	Othene Bell	Ongoing	Continue to survey students biannually.
	M. Lindbloom	Ongoing	Review the emphasis of athletic and non-athletic activities to determine the level of lifelong activities.
4.2.6 Ensure that all Student Support programs assist students in meeting their academic needs.	Othene Bell Greg Fancher	Spring each year	Board report of time spent by activity for counselors.
4.2.7 Work with parents to decrease television viewing time among all segments of our students.	Reading Foundation & Principals	Ongoing	Continue process already established.
4.2.8 Increase parents' involvement in the selection of appropriate classroom teachers for their children.	Principals	Nov 98	Report on current practice.
	Principals	May 99	Report on plans for increased parental involvement for 98-99.
4.2.9 Increase parental authentic participation in District problem-solving, in parent-teacher conferences, and in the classrooms at all levels.	Principals	98-99	Each school develop a parent involvement plan. Include procedures to get parents information prior to involvement in specific activities. (See bldg. Customer Focus Plans).

Action	Responsible	Date	Measure/Activity
4.2.10 In time expand to thirty percent (30%) the number of parents and community members on the Curriculum Advisory Committee.	M. Lindbloom	Jan 98	Continue parent involvement grant - Washington Mutual at selected sites. Report
4.2.11 Develop a staff profile that baselines essential professional knowledge and instructional skills criteria which can be used to validate and continue progress toward a "world-class" level of learning and instruction	Jim Verhulp	May 99 97-2000 Fall	Develop baseline profile of staff degrees; majors and minors. Develop parameters for profile database. Provide PSR training for all staff. Provide classroom management training for new staff and those identified in need.
4.2.12 Using our profile, develop a marketing plan to recruit and retain staff members with globally competitive skills.	Jim Verhulp	Ongoing	Recruiting trips to Washington colleges. Advertisements in publications that target ethnic minority applicants. Recruit at Career Fair in Spokane in May.
4.2.13 In cooperation with families and our community, develop the attitude in students that "with work I can succeed."	Elem. & M.S. Principals Linda Cameron	98-2000	Poster campaign for halls and classrooms.
4.2.14 Encourage student service to the community	Othene Bell Dottie Stevens	97-2000	Continue to develop Service Learning plan at Kennewick HS for District model.
4.2.15 Dialogue with members of different faiths and ethnic groups regarding acceptable concepts to teach in schools, including qualities and ethics needed for employment, citizenship, family membership and others consistent with the adult roles established by the District, parents, and community.	Paul Rosier	Ongoing	Hold regular meetings with clergy, parents, ethnic minority groups and others to gain their views. Engage the community in creating a "safe schools" plan.

GOAL #5. ENSURE THAT THE DISTRICT IS EFFICIENTLY OPERATED AND FISCALLY SOUND.

SUBGOAL	PERSON	DUE	INDICATOR
5.1 Create and maintain over the next 7 years a series of financial management reports which monitor critical financial area and which encourage innovation.	Business Mngr.	Ongoing	Provide the comprehensive "4 page" report of funds and expenditures.
	Paul Rosier	Aug 98 & 99	Report efforts to seek additional resources from public and private agencies to continue partnerships, programs that benefit the students of Kennewick.
	Business Mngr.	Sept 98	Report cost and funding source of negotiated contract changes projected over next 10 years.
	Business Mngr.	June 98+	Report on the annual employee cost-saving suggest program 10.9.
	Business Mngr.	Mar 98+	Report if rental of designated district facilities is commensurate with the costs of operation.
	Business Mngr.	Mar 98+	Report on replacement schedule for major capital expenditures.
	Business Mngr.	Mar 98+	Report on student counts per building. Report on five (5) year preventive maintenance schedule.
5.2 By 1999, establish a fund-balance-contingency reserve of 5% of the total general fund budget.	Business Mngr.	Ongoing	Maintain at least a 5% fund-balance.
5.3 Create a standing-ten-member-financial-review committee.	Business Mngr.	Ongoing	Proposed makeup and agenda for regular meetings. Approval of yearly agenda and membership. Presentation to Board.
5.4 Encourage school and District entrepreneurial enterprises.			On hold

GOAL #6 ENSURE THAT THE DECISION-MAKING GOVERNANCE, AND COLLECTIVE BARGAINING PROCESSES WITHIN THE DISTRICT WILL ALWAYS FOCUS ON THE BEST INTEREST OF STUDENTS.

SUBGOAL	PERSON	DUE	INDICATOR
6.1 The interests of the students are clearly defined apart from the interests of the affected adults in each major decision. All decisions strive to reflect the best interests of children while optimizing the interests of adults, community, and the institution. Decisions which benefit adults and may adversely affect students must be justified by compelling reasons.	Paul Rosier Cabinet	Each Spring / June 1998	Continue to develop a focused collaborative process with staff. / Annual report to the Board.
6.2 Annually identify and realign the structure and objectives of every district committee to the Strategic Plan.	M. Lindbloom Paul Rosier	Nov 98 / Feb 98	Listing of committees, members, budget, projected person hours, and objectives. / Concept paper on recommendations.
6.3 Decision making within the District level will involve, as much as possible, all stake-holders including staff, students, parents, and community members and will occur at the level closest to those affected by the decision	Paul Rosier	Ongoing	Continue the District Shared Decision Making Task Force. Implementation of the shared decision making concepts at volunteer schools. Increase number of schools by 3.
6.4 Decision making occurs in an atmosphere of mutual respect permitting a vigorous exchange on the merits of ideas without intrusion of personalities or privileged points of view.	Paul Rosier	Each Spring	Cite examples in a Board Report indicating that the content and the spirit of this indicator are being met.
6.5 Employ "Win-Win" bargaining with all labor groups.	Jim Verhulp	Ongoing / LTM Meetings	Open dialogue with the Union officials related to student, staff, and school needs. / Monthly data collection and dialogue with Directors, Principals, Supervisors, related to student and staff needs.
6.6 Annually review and revise the Strategic Plan.	Paul Rosier	Ongoing	Annual planning meeting. / Report to the Board on a quarterly basis.

GOAL #7 ENCOURAGE INNOVATION AND FLEXIBILITY THROUGHOUT THE DISTRICT'S OPERATION.

SUBGOAL	PERSON	DUE	INDICATOR
7.1 Develop a user-friendly method for staff to access resources to increase efficiency and/or higher academic achievement.	Paul Rosier	Ongoing	Inform staff through staff update of activities.
7.2 Evaluate the effectiveness of this venture.	Paul Rosier	Ongoing	Develop graphic Strategic Plan report system for Board Room.
7.3 Seek system solutions to leverage change in the system.	Paul Rosier	Ongoing	More course choice at middle school. Multiple diplomas at the high school. Flexible primary structure. Performance-based initiatives.

GOAL #8. ESTABLISH A GOAL FOR EXPECTED STUDENT PERFORMANCE ON THE CERTIFICATE OF MASTERY ASSESMENT TEST.

SUBGOAL	PERSON	DUE	INDICATOR
8.1 Establish a goal for the 10th grade test to be achieved by 2004.	Paul Rosier Principals	Fall 98	Engage the high school staff in setting goal. Goal established and adopted by the Board.
8.2 Establish student performance targets for the 4th and 7th grade tests.	Directors Principals	Fall 98	Engage the elementary and middle staff in establishing the targets.
8.3 Develop instructional strategies and programs to assist student to meet the performance standards at 4th, 7th, & 10th grades.	M. Lindbloom Bev Henderson Othene Bell Greg Fancher	98-99	Focus staff development using per diem days, implement CORE and First Steps reading strategies and training. Implement Six Traits reading training for MS and HS teachers.
8.4 Develop strategies, programs and alternatives for students who fail to meet the criteria on the 4th 7th, & 10th grade tests.	M. Lindbloom Directors Principals	98-2000	Increase summer school enrollment options. Review the literature on successful remediation approaches.
8.5 Develop a district-wide plan to inform parents and community patrons of the State Standards & Assessment and the expectations of Kennewick School District.	Linda Cameron Paul Rosier	98-2000	Organize a communication plan. Present plan for Board approval.

Appendix F

Decoding Language:
Whole Language for Meaning, Phonetics,
and Phonological Awareness

In our district, the extremists on both ends of the phonics/whole language continuum are fairly quiet. It is not *whether* whole language, phonological awareness, or phonetics, but *how much* of each and *when*. The phonic advocates who focus exclusively on repetitive drill have been subdued as the value of quality texts and intrinsically meaningful tasks becomes evident. The sometimes vitriolic denial by whole-language practitioners of the value and practice of skills instruction, including phonetic practices, has been moderated by the convergence of nation-wide research during the last five years on its significant value in early reading acquisition. Here's a very brief overview of the current position on how we decode language.

The whole-language approach originated from the work of Ken Goodman in the seventies with "look-say" being an earlier precursor. It focuses on teaching initial reading skills from the contextual clues provided in a symbol-rich environment of literature, poetry, and stories. Its primary focus is on the meta-context of meaning in which reading occurs. The mechanics of phonetics, when taught, are imbedded in the context of stories, discussions, and predictable texts.

Phonics is the process of teaching the imperfect correlation between the twenty-six English alphabet symbols and the forty-plus sounds English uses. Known as the alphabet principle or "breaking the code," explicit phonetic instruction is the repetitive task of learning most of the common letters and sounds and applying this skill with controlled vocabularies where the rules work.

Phonological awareness is the awareness and ability to distinguish distinct sounds in oral language. These include the forty-two to forty-four distinct phonemes used in English as well as combinations of sounds larger than single phonemes. Phonological research is a relative newcomer, with most of the research having been done in the last three decades. On a primitive level, it is measured by a child's ability to hear rhymes. More advanced skills include hearing alliterations, blending tasks, segmentation tasks, and adding or deleting phonemes to words. Phonemic awareness is not phonetics and it is not mere auditory discrimination.

Phonemic awareness is the most potent predictor of success in learning to read. It is more positively correlated to reading than tests of general intelligence, reading readiness, and listening comprehension.[1]

Phonemes are crucial in learning the English alphabetic system or how print represents spoken words. If children cannot hear and manipulate the sounds in spoken words,

---

[1] Linda Diamond and Sheila Mandel of the Consortium on Reading Excellence, *Building a Powerful Reading Program: From Research to Practice* (Sacramento: California Education Policy Seminar/California State University Institute for Education Reform, February 1996), 3, citing Stanovich 1986, 1994.

they have an extremely difficult time learning how to map those sounds to letters and letter patterns—the essence of decoding. Phonemic awareness "is the most important core and causal factor separating normal and disabled readers."[2] Naturally, phonemic awareness also strongly impacts learning to spell.

Phonemic awareness in pre-school, kindergarten, and early first grade includes the ability:

- To hear rhymes or alliteration
- To blend sounds to make a word: /a/+/t/ = at
- To count phonemes in words: "How many sounds do you hear in *is*?"
- To identify the beginning, middle, and final sounds in words
- To substitute one phoneme for another: change the /h/ in "hot" to /p/
- To delete phonemes from words: omit the /c/ from "cat"

Early research of the U.S. Office of Education Cooperative Research Program in First-Grade Reading Instruction (1964-67) identified the three best predictors of success in early reading as (1) prereaders' ability to recognize and name uppercase and lowercase letters, (2) prereaders' ability to discriminate phonemes auditorily, and (3) IQ.[3]

Adams suggests that it is not merely the accuracy with which prereaders perform these tasks but the ease or fluency with which they do. The two best phonemic discriminators appear to be the phoneme segmentation (mat = m/a/t/), phoneme manipulation ("Say hill without the *h*"), and blending (/m/a/p/ = map).

The predictive and correlative strength of letter recognition facility and phonemic awareness bears reflection for two reasons. The first reason is that the very potency of these two skills reinforces the hypothesis that budding familiarity with letter-to-sound relations is invaluable to the beginning reader. The second is that, as predictors of reading acquisition, there is something strange about them.

Specifically, it is not clear how either letter recognition fluency or phonemic segmentation skills could be acquired except through their instruction and exercise. What, then do they tell us about reading readiness? One irrepressible interpretation is that the likelihood that a child will succeed in the first grade depends most of all on how much she or he has already learned about reading before getting there—and this interpretation seems soberingly correct.[4]

It has been our observation that the best programs use it all: assuring phonological abilities thorough phonetic mastery including inventive and normal spelling, and cognitive engagement in writing, reading, and discussions which engender a love of the process in the student. The best programs use their time first and lavishly for reading. They encourage strategies based on specific student need and avoid lock-step teaching strategies that are too easy for the advanced students of the class and too difficult for the struggling students.

---

[2] Marilyn Jager Adams, *Beginning to Read: Thinking and Learning about Print* (Cambridge, MA: MIT Press, 1990).

[3] Ibid., 55-81.

[4] Ibid., 82.

APPENDIX G

Model State Reading Accountability Legislation

Note: This model legislation contains specific dates and assumes passage in the spring of 2001, with a 90% goal and a four-year target. It also assumes that testing and establishing each building's reading baseline will occur in the spring of 2002, with reporting commencing in the spring of 2003. The definition of terms in Section 3 has remained as Section 3 but has been moved to the end of the bill for ease in reading.

AN ACT Relating to reading accountability: adding new sections to chapter_____; creating new sections; and making an appropriation.

BE IT ENACTED BY THE LEGISLATURE OF THE STATE OF _____:

NEW SECTION. Sec. 1. The legislature finds that it is essential for children in the public schools to read early and well in elementary school. The legislature further finds that a clear and visible goal, assessments to determine the reading level at each building, annual measurements of elementary school reading improvement, and creating accountability in each level of the educational system will result in a significant increase in the number of children reading at or above grade level.

NEW SECTION. Sec. 2. This act may be known and cited as "the reading accountability act."

NEW SECTION. Sec. 3. (at the end of this section)

NEW SECTION. Sec. 4. A new section is added to chapter ____ to read as follows:

The reading goal of Chapter _____ Laws of 2001 (this act) is: By the year 2006 and each year thereafter 90% or more of all of this state's public school third graders will read at or above grade level, by the end of their third grade year.

NEW SECTION. Sec. 5. A new section is added to chapter ____ to read as follows:

To achieve the state reading goal:

(1) Each school district shall use classroom-based assessments to evaluate the reading level of its kindergarten, first, and second graders annually for purposes of intervention and remediation commencing in the spring of 2002.

(2) Each school district shall assess the reading level of its third graders in the spring of 2002 and each year thereafter using the third-grade assessment for the primary purpose of system accountability and not primarily for the purpose of remediation commencing at grade four.

(3) Each elementary school shall determine its building baseline which shall be its actual percentage of students reading at or above third-grade level as determined by the third-grade reading assessment administered in the spring of 2002.

(4) Each public elementary school building is expected to make equal annual incremental improvement from its baseline. Equal annual incremental improvement is one fourth of the reading improvement necessary to progress from the building baseline in the spring of 2002 to the state reading goal of 90% in the spring of 2006 and shall be calculated and measured on a building by building basis. The percentage of required improvement will be different for different public schools since it is based on the individual building baselines.

NEW SECTION. Sec. 6. A new section is added to chapter ____ to read as follows:

The levels of system accountability and reporting necessary to achieve the reading goal shall include the state, the professional associations, the principals, the teachers, the public school buildings, the school districts, and the parents.

(1) The superintendent of public instruction or the superintendent's designee shall:

(a) report annually to the house and senate education committees on the statewide progress toward the reading goal;

(b) provide progress reports on the third-grade reading assessment scores to the public in clear, understandable terms on a building, district, and statewide basis, and disclose the number of third graders reading at each grade-level equivalent across the range from kindergarten through eighth grade;

(c) encourage buildings to develop a repertoire of instructional approaches tailored to different student learning styles;

(d) provide information to public schools and school districts regarding organizational and instructional practices of representative buildings that are making or exceeding the equal annual incremental improvement toward the reading goal;

(e) not adopt a specific instructional approach. The standard for evaluating an elementary school on a district's reading instruction will be whether it results in annual and incremental growth.

(2) The Office of the Superintendent of Public Instruction shall coordinate the activities of relevant professional associations. It shall:

(a) Meet and confer with each relevant professional association regarding voluntary alignment of association resources to support the achievement of the reading goal;

(b) report annually to the Senate and House education committees on the efforts of professional associations to support the achievement of the reading goal;

(3) Each public elementary school principal shall have the primary responsibility within the building for providing leadership in reaching the reading goal.

(4) Each third-grade teacher shall annually report to the parent or guardian the reading level of his or her child as measured by the third-grade reading assessment commencing June 2002 and each year thereafter in grade-level equivalents.

(5) Each public elementary school shall annually report to its community the number, the actual percentage, and the adjusted percentage of third-grade students reading at or above third-grade level and the distribution and range of all reading scores in grade-level equivalents increments, on the third-grade reading assessment required under section 4 of this act.

(6) Each district shall report to the superintendent of public instruction annually beginning October 2001, the number, the actual percentage, and adjusted percentage of third-grade students reading at or above grade level on the third-grade reading assessment required under section 5 of this act.

(7) Parents are a child's first and most influential teacher. Public school districts shall provide encouragement and support for parents to read with their children at least 20 minutes a day from birth through third grade.

NEW SECTION. Sec. 7. A new section is added to chapter _____ to read as follows:

Nothing in this act shall be construed to provide a cause of legal action for damages or specific performance.

NEW SECTION. Sec. 8. If any provision of this act or its application to any person or circumstance is held invalid, the remainder of the act or the application of the provision to other persons or circumstances is not affected.

NEW SECTION. Sec. 3. A new section is added to chapter _____ to read as follows:

The definitions in this section apply throughout sections 1 through 8 of this act unless the context clearly requires otherwise.

(1) "Actual percentage" means the headcount enrollment of third-grade students reading at or above third-grade level divided by the headcount enrollment of third-grade students in the building on the date the third-grade reading assessment is administered.

(2) "Adjusted percentage" means the actual percentage minus those students who were not in the district at least one-half of each of the student's second- and third-grade years, and minus those students who have been enrolled in a bilingual program for two or less years from both the numerator and denominator.

(3) "At or above third-grade level" means at or above the grade-level equivalent standard established for the test.

(4) "Building baseline" means the building's actual percentage in the spring of 2002.

(5) "Equal annual incremental improvement" is one fourth of the improvement necessary to progress from the building baseline to the reading goal by the spring of 2006 and is calculated as follows: The state goal of 90% less the building baseline divided by four.

(6) "Factored equal annual incremental improvement" is calculated as follows: The state goal of 90% less the building's adjusted percentage in the spring of 2001 divided by four.

(7) "Reading goal" means 90 percent of a public elementary school building's annual headcount enrollment of third-grade students reading at or above grade level as measured in grade-level equivalence by the third-grade reading assessment.

(8) "Third-grade reading assessment" means the reading portion of the third-grade California Test of Basic Skills, or the reading subtest of such other standardized achievement test given annually to all students in grade three pursuant to _____.

About the Authors

Lynn Fielding is in his twelfth year as a director of the Kennewick Board of Education and in his second term as one of eleven directors of the Washington State School Directors Association (WSSDA). He is the State Senate appointee to Washington's Professional Education Advisory Committee (PEAC). He and his wife, Wendy Gilbert Fielding, a former second-grade schoolteacher, are the parents of four children. A business attorney with an LL.M. in taxation from Georgetown University, Washington, D.C., he also farms in Adams County with his eighty-year-old parents.

Nancy Kerr is president of the Reading Foundation. She has served in numerous district and state positions, including as a former Kennewick School Board Director, as co-chair of the Citizens' Levy and Bond committee since 1988, and high school teacher. She was honored with the 1992 Washington State Crystal Apple Award for service to education, the 1998 Washington State Literacy Award of the International Reading Association, and America Reads Challenge Leadership Recognition from the U.S. Department of Education. She and her husband, Leland, have four children.

Paul Rosier is the superintendent of Kennewick (Washington) School District (14,000 students). Other administrative positions in his twenty-eight-year career include being superintendent of Mesa County Valley School District in Grand Junction, Colorado, (18,000 students) and of Page (Arizona) Unified School District (3,000 students). Rosier's doctoral dissertation in 1977 focused on initial reading strategies which moved Navajo children at Rock Point, Arizona, from the 30-35th percentile to the 50th percentile, an increase equivalent to two grades. He and his wife, Mary, a curriculum specialist with the Educational Service District 123 in Pasco, have three children.

INDEX